"*Forty Voices* creates lifughs through true accounts of  lives of young people. Every stel of faith. If you're about to gratulations in advance."

—Jonathan Sprinkles, age 26
Author, *Why Settle? Be the Best YOU That YOU Can Be!* and *Get the Fire Back! 99 Ways to Restore Purpose and Passion to Your Life*

"Nothing fires up a young person for Christ like another young person fired up for Christ! *Forty Voices* is a devotional by young people for young people. It's challenging, inspiring and guaranteed to motivate you to know and be more and more like Jesus. *Forty Voices* will rock your world!"

—Ben Naitoko, Youth Pastor, Mackay Christian Family, Australia

"Reading about the triumphs young people have experienced through God and His grace inspires me to remain strong in my faith and shows me how much God has truly blessed me in life! This book is full of these wonderful devotionals!"

—Aileen Fitzpatrick, age 19, Texas

"It is my great joy to recommend this devotional guide. Brad Huddleston and Josh Sundquist not only love the Lord but they are both effective communicators of His love. They have asked forty young people from around the word to partner with them in this project, and I am looking forward to what God is going to do through their effort."

—Evangelist Steve Wingfield

Thanks for sharing your
Story! It will bless many
People...

Brian Hamilton

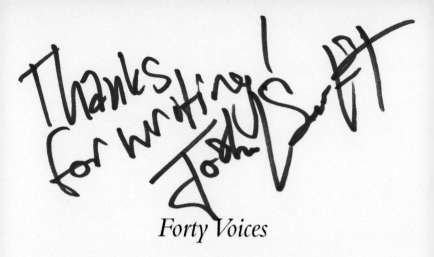

Forty Voices

Stories of Hope from Our Generation

Brad Huddleston, Brian Hamilton,
and Josh Sundquist

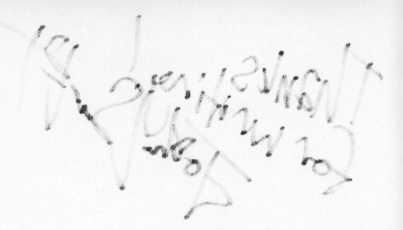

Forty Voices: Stories of Hope from Our Generation

Published by Hats Off Books™
610 E. Delano Street, Suite 104
Tucson, Arizona 85705, U.S.A.
www.hatsoffbooks.com

International Standard Book Number: 1-58736-263-5
Library of Congress Control Number: 2003096921

This book is dedicated to the forty young people from around the world who share their hearts on the pages within.

Acknowledgements

The authors of this book would like to humbly and gratefully acknowledge: Belinda Barker for letting us use her conference room at Geotechnical & Environmental Services, Inc., for our insane twelve-hour whirlwind editing session; our friend, fellow writer, fellow HHS grad, and all-around good guy Ben Lamb for coming up with the title for this book; Heather Horner, Crystal Campbell, and Brian Charette were all invaluable in their editing suggestions; all of the fantastic people who work for Hats Off Books, especially AnnMarie MacKinnon for her belief in the project and helpful cooperation throughout, and Suzanne Haws for her incredibly efficient editing and constant professionalism; Dan Hammer and Robbie Thompson for their help in getting the word out about *Forty Voices*; the makers of Sweet Breath breath freshener that allowed Brian and Josh to share the same microphone during our radio spots; all forty of the fantastic young people who took the time and energy to share their hearts with the world through this book—it would've never happened without you and we love you all—and most of all, our Lord and Savior Jesus Christ, for whom all the glory is reserved.

Contents

The *Forty Voices* Story

Joshua Sundquist

In some ways, the story of this book started ten years ago when a little boy was diagnosed with cancer. A disc jockey for a Christian radio station started receiving phone calls asking for prayer for the little boy. Soon the little boy and the disc jockey met and became friends, and together they trusted God as the boy fought and beat the cancer. About nine years later, the disc jockey emailed the little boy (who had since grown into a handsome young bachelor) and proposed writing a devotional together.

The little boy/handsome young bachelor? That's me. The disc jockey? That's Brad Huddleston.

Although I first told Brad I was too busy to write a devotional, God soon gave me the idea for an anthology written by young people from around the world. I called Brad, as well as my high school buddy, Brian Hamilton, and they both agreed to join the project. So there we were: two eighteen-year-olds and a middle-aged disc jockey, off to change the world.

It wasn't long before we realized that God had put us together with careful design. Brian, who started his own Web-design business in high school, designed a stellar website to collect the devotionals, and wrote Web-based programs to speed up the production process. Brad, who was by now an evangelist as well as a radio guy, had the mass-media platform to get the word out about our project and ask for submissions. And me? Well, I'd been trying (unsuccessfully) to get an autobiography published for almost two years. They say that failure is the greatest teacher, and indeed, by now I knew enough about book publishing to get this devotional from idea to paper in about six months.

And there you have it: The Legend of the Forty Voices. (Please feel free to adapt/embellish this legend however you want, should you choose to relate it to your children someday.)

What Can I Expect from *Forty Voices*?

Brian Hamilton

Growing up can be a tumultuous experience, especially in a culture that discourages heartfelt sharing. As youth, it can be hard to know whether anybody has ever felt what we are feeling right now, or whether a loving God could possibly be behind this horrible event, or whether a recent turn of events in our favor was evidence of a god. It's hard to understand the world from our experience alone, and sometimes it's hard to find someone to share the world with.

That's why *Forty Voices*, that's why youth stories. Every youth in this book has experienced God and recognized his or her experience as being of God. We wanted to show the youth of the world that other people *are* going through the same things that they are, and that God *does* live in everything that happens. Each story intends to demonstrate how God manifests Himself to us through our experiences, and works in our hearts and minds to change us into the people He wants us to be.

Christianity is a faith based on action. We are called to actively love, live, and praise in every moment of our lives. In these stories, people just like you are laying bare their encounters with God, the times that they have actively loved (or failed to love, and learned from it), the testing moments that God has used to teach them. We all come across similar obstacles and comforts in life; *Forty Voices* aims to help you recognize the experiences for what they are, and to help you think through how to react in difficult situations before you encounter them.

To help you better connect with the authors and their stories, we've provided a section in the back of the book full of writer profiles. Most of the authors added some extra information about themselves (some serious, some not so serious) to make it easier for you to understand the background of the person behind the story. Some even provided their contact information, so you can get to know them personally if you want.

Our experiences help shape who we are; we learn from them and we grow from them. Reading about other people's experiences can have an equally profound impact. Read, learn, grow.

How to Get the Most Out of This Book

Brad Huddleston

There are basically two ways to read a book. You can fly through it or you can take some time to "mine it." I hope you'll take some time to do some digging while in this devotional. Here are some suggestions that will help you get the most out of this book.

- Set aside time to be quiet. You'll have to create this environment and it won't be easy. Shut off both your regular and cell phones and let your answering machine take messages. Shut off other things such as your computer and television. Go to a place where no one can find you except your parent(s) or a friend. Be willing to have people get irritated at you when they can't reach you.

- Consider your time with God more important than time you spend with friends.

- Keep a *New International Version* (NIV) Bible handy as you go through *Forty Voices*. The reason is because we used this particular version when editing the book and it's easy to understand.

- As you find verses in the book, mark the same ones in your own Bible. Allow yourself to read more than one verse should you come across others that are interesting.

- Have an attitude of expectancy that God is going to speak to you as you read. This will be enhanced if you'll spend some time talking to God before you begin.

- In your prayer time, don't do all of the talking. Even though you probably won't hear God speak to you with your physical ears, trust that He is speaking directly to your heart.

- Finally, some people find it helpful to keep a journal. Write things that God speaks to your heart as you read the Bible and *Forty Voices*. Journals are particularly good to read during those "dry times" when you're having trouble hearing from God.

DAY 1

He who has ears, let him hear.

Matthew 11:15

The church was clearing after the regular Sunday service. I was about to leave when I felt a tug on my sleeve.

"John, I don't know what to do...." It was Amy, a friend I'd known for a few months. Dark mascara streamed from her hazel-green eyes.

I put my hand on her shoulder. "What's going on?"

She reached into her purse and pulled out a sonogram. Amy was pregnant at seventeen.

Las Vegas has the highest teen pregnancy rate, teen suicide/attempted suicide rate, and high-school drop-out rate in the United States. Amy fits all three of those categories. She came from a broken family and tried to find love in alcohol, hard drugs, and men. Word on the street was that Amy was "easy," so unknown guys would often knock on her door.

She clenched the sonogram hard. "I just didn't want to be alone, John." She kept repeating, "I just didn't want to be alone."

I hugged her. "I know, Amy. I know."

We sat down in the near-empty auditorium and she detailed the "double life" she described herself as leading. One Amy was a clean-cut church girl who sang in the worship team. The other Amy led a much darker life. She relayed the entire sequence of choices she had made to arrive at this point. The details were difficult to listen to, but as any friend would, I simply listened.

We talked several more times during her pregnancy. Well, actually she talked for the majority of our conversations. I simply listened. She told me about the Alcoholics Anonymous meetings she went to, her therapist, and how much both were helping. The more she told me about her life, the more she started to come to grips with her past. With the help of a parenting course she took at church, she was genuinely excited to bring her daughter into the world.

Rachel was born a nine-pound, perfectly healthy child with stunning, beaming blue eyes. Her only hair was on the back of her head and it shot straight into the air. A beautiful baby with a radiant future.

Months later, when I held Rachel, Amy looked me so deeply in the eye I thought she'd bump into my soul. "Thank you, John."

"For what?"

"For being there for me. You've helped me through some of the toughest times of my life. You've been a wonderful friend."

At that moment I realized that simply listening—listening without passing judgment or even giving advice—can be more beneficial than speaking volumes of time-tested wisdom or employing the strongest of leadership principles. Through Amy's deepest pain and greatest joy, all I did was listen to her.

Yesterday I received a wedding invitation from Amy. She's getting hitched to a loving, supportive military man. Oh, and Rachel just took her first steps!

Simply listen. You'll make a huge difference.

DAY 2

ELIZABETH, AGE 20

Heal me, O LORD, and I will be healed; save me and I will be saved, for you are the one I praise.

Jeremiah 17:14

The day I left for college, I started crying. I was leaving my family, my friends, and my home to go to a completely foreign place. But just when I thought things couldn't get any more depressing, I received the worst phone call of my life. It was my sister, the powerful professional who could hold the world together from her desk in downtown D.C. She was scared and sobbing.

My sister told me what I already knew: another of my sisters, a brilliant and creative woman, was slowly losing her mind. The time had come for us to decide whether our sister's suicidal tendencies warranted committing her to a mental hospital. After a painful examination of the evidence, we agreed not to commit her as long as she agreed to certain protective measures. Too far away to touch these two women I loved, I hung up the phone.

With my heart searing and tears gushing, I raced to my InterVarsity chapter's freshman retreat. We began with worship on campus. I hid in the darkness of the falling night screaming silent hatred at the God who had created my sister and then allowed her mind and body to separate. I hated Him even more for stranding me on that forsaken night.

In the midst of my rage, I glanced down just long enough to notice Beth leading worship in her knee brace. I knew her story. She had been a promising varsity athlete until the accident that destroyed her knee left her condemned never to walk without a brace, never to run again. God had allowed her to fall from a future in sports to a physical handicap. I realized that if she could not just praise God but lead InterVarsity worship after all that, I could stave off my hatred of Him long enough to mumble a few lines.

I spent the rest of that weekend learning of God's plan and provision for my life. Beth's enthusiasm had been just the boost I needed to soften my heart, and I listened intently to every word the speakers said. I knew that I had to tell Beth what her wordless testimony had accomplished, but being too ashamed to speak with her, I hid a note in her knee brace while she slept. Of course, she found me out.

That Thursday we had lunch together, shared our stories, and began a journey through Jeremiah to meet Jehovah-rapha, the God who heals. Together we learned that God, like a surgeon, may allow pain, but that pain is always purposeful and effective.

Sixteen months and a thousand prayers later, with my sister safely home and thriving, I cried tears of joy as I cheered Beth over the last hill of her first triathlon. God, in

His love and His own time, had done the impossible. He had healed my sister's mind, Beth's body, and, hardest of all, my grieving, hateful heart.

DAY 3

BETH, AGE 23

Fear not, for I have redeemed you: I have summoned you by name; you are mine. When you pass through the waters, I will be with you; and when you pass through the rivers, they will not sweep over you. When you walk through the fire, you will not be burned; the flames will not set you ablaze.

Isaiah 43:1b-2

On the outside, I was a typical college student. I appeared carefree, energetic, and somewhat rebellious. On the inside, however, I was drowning in sadness and loneliness. A product of child abuse and a broken home, I could tell true stories to rival those on daytime television. But most of the time, I kept the stories to myself and worked very hard to keep up the mask of "normal, happy, successful college student."

During October of my freshman year, I was at a conference when I felt God calling me to summer missions. At first I thought that was crazy and I tried to talk God out of it. "But God," I said, "I can't be a missionary! It's taking every drop of energy in me just to keep myself going from day to day. I just don't have anything to offer other people."

The voices of friends and family all around me seemed to agree. My boyfriend at the time said I was being emotional and irrational. "You should stay here and earn money this summer. Working for free is a waste of time," he argued. My mother agreed with him. "What's left of your family needs you," she reminded me. "Stay here and spend time with us." Even my former youth minister had words of caution. "Are you sure you are up to this?" he asked.

Yet when December came, I found myself turning in my summer missions' application. I figured I had nothing to lose since I knew they wouldn't choose me anyway. "They're sure to throw out my application at first glance," I rationalized. After interviews in March, however, I received a phone call inviting me to go to the mission field I had listed as my first choice, a home for abandoned children. Again, I was faced with a decision. Should I step out on faith and go where God appeared to be sending me? Or should I take the rational road by staying home and earning money? I didn't actually *have* any money, and I wasn't sure how I would pay my tuition or bills for the upcoming semester. For some reason, though, I decided to do it. It may have been faith, but it was probably my rebellious desire to prove everyone else wrong. But whatever the reason, I found myself terrified as I followed God out of my comfort zone into unknown territory.

The eleven weeks that followed turned out to be the best time of my life. For the first time ever, I felt like I was exactly where God wanted me to be. As I poured myself into those hurting kids, I found that I was no longer drowning in sadness. The mask I had struggled to keep up for so long had finally melted into a real smile. And you know what? When I went back to school in the fall, much to the astonishment of my boyfriend, somehow the bills all got paid.

DAY 4

BEN, AGE 18

King will reply, 'I tell you the truth, whatever you did for one of the least of these brothers of mine, you did for me.'
Matthew 25:40

When I sat next to him at the table, I thought I was doing a good deed sitting next to the disfigured, most likely incoherent, man in a wheelchair whose right eyeball was a plastic prosthetic. He started talking to me and sure enough, his slurred pronunciation required dedicated listening.

For the sake of attempting conversation though, I asked, "How's the food?"

With a trace of humor, he replied, "Thought I was going to get a hotdog, but instead I got a colddog!"

I chuckled at his reference to the food's temperature. He seemed to be a friendly fellow. So I opened myself up to him by explaining why I was here—doing a service program through the Mennonite church and on Tuesday nights, our team volunteered at this free diner for those in need of food.

To my surprise, this man with a handicap, Gary, could relate to me; he had been raised in a Mennonite family and church, done a year of service work, and went to a Christian college. Hearing bits of his life story, I discovered the many hardships of Gary's life: as a young boy, he accidentally shot his eye with a BB gun; as a teenage athlete, he broke many bones; at twenty-seven, he was paralyzed in a near-fatal car accident that left doctors questioning whether he would ever be more than a vegetable. And yet, after all these calamities, he said to me with a twinkle in his one real eye, "Only by God's grace do I live today."

He majored in psychology, a major I have intermittently considered, and we both listened to the same type of music. We both valued a sense of humor in rough times and we even shared some of the same mannerisms. Almost startlingly, our lives were similar.

Why God lets me use both my legs while others like Gary cannot move below the waist—I don't know. But I do know why the Holy Spirit nudged me to sit next to Gary, who was eating cooked squash turned cold. That night, I had to witness God's truth, that all people, mobile by feet or by wheels, disfigured or not, have a life story just as dynamic and complex as mine, including peaks of spiritual heights and valleys of misfortune or depression. And the sum total of six billion people on this planet, each with their matchless stories and formative pasts, reveals the infinite wonder of God's mysterious creativity.

In some way, I can identify with every person alive, like I did with Gary, which leads to having compassion for people and then to the genuine want to help others by service. Woefully, so many people need Christian compassion and charity, such as those who live in the constant reality of hardships, hunger, spiritual poverty, and having no shelter and no comfort to turn to.

I verbally thanked Gary for the talk while my mind praised him for the epiphany. I felt bad that his soup cooled even more during our nonstop conversing. After the exchanging of good-byes, I started to think: maybe I could reflect and serve Christ's truth by volunteering at disability hospitals or rehabilitation centers. The possibilities for showing His love to "the least of these" are endless.

DAY 5

RACHEL, AGE 24

Trust in the Lord with all your heart and lean not on your own understanding; in all your ways acknowledge Him, and He will make your paths straight.

Proverbs 3:5-6

Two young teenagers meet for a night of fun with no limits. The fun goes a little too far that night. Now the girl is pregnant. What can she do? She could keep the child, and be unfit to mother it at her very young age. She could abort the child, the convenient thing to do. Or she could give her child up for adoption. As she is pondering this decision, there is a Christian couple praying and waiting for a child, trusting God to provide.

This same child, in the arms of her adoptive parents, is inflicted with a severe case of pneumonia at three months old. Fragile, unable to breathe on her own, she is placed in an oxygen tent with little hope. Her mother prays for her, trusting God to heal, and sees a glowing light come down from the ceiling, fill up the tent, and heal her baby girl.

Now the baby girl is grown up and she's driving her car cautiously on a rural West Virginia road because of the rainy weather. Control of the car is lost, and it spins around until the force drives it into a gigantic tree. This tree rips through the middle of the car, and now it is all that is holding the car over a cliff, keeping it from falling.

I remember the moment I was on a stretcher in the back of the ambulance. I felt very fragile and vulnerable. And right there, for the first time in my life, I allowed myself to feel completely open with God. It was at that moment that I fully submitted all to Him. I knew that even when I was a baby who was put up for adoption and then almost died of pneumonia, God had his hand on me. Now, two decades later, I finally realized all I could do was trust.

In the six months before the accident, it seemed that every layer of my life was being peeled open by God. He was showing me my lack of trust in Him regarding each layer. It started with my desire for a godly man to marry; continued with my finances; my future life and ministry; my health; family issues; relationships problems; financial supply for ministry efforts; ultimately, my life. I have come to the slow realization that I had trusted Jesus Christ with my soul for eternal salvation and everlasting life, but had not trusted Him with the rest of my life. I had lost touch with what He commands in Proverbs 3:5-6.

Trust is very easy to break, and very difficult to build. I know more so now than ever before that God will not do anything to break my trust. My life, literally, is in His hands. Sometimes when people do things to break our trust, we are so hesitant to give it again. But God has proven Himself trustworthy!

Do you trust Him? God wants all of your trust, not just one area of it. When we trust Him, we acknowledge Him for who He is.

In God we trust, amen.

DAY 6

NICOLE, AGE 16

Get rid of all bitterness, rage and anger, brawling and slander, along with every form of malice. Be kind and compassionate to one another, forgiving each other, just as in Christ God forgave you.

Ephesians 4:31-32

I have a good guy friend. There's no special relationship between us. I've just known David for what seems like forever. Besides that, his family lives two houses away from mine, so we manage to see each other quite a lot.

One day after youth group we were talking together, and he asked me to go to the winter formal dance at the high school with him, just as friends. I agreed. I thought it would be fun to go with him and a group of other friends. I excitedly began planning.

The big day finally came, and I felt so elegant in my long blue gown. The evening started out well. We danced together for a while, and everybody seemed to be having fun.

"Is it okay if I dance with some other girls for a while?" David asked.

"Sure," I replied nonchalantly. After all, we had only gone together as friends. I left to find a group of girls to chat with. About an hour later, I started wandering around the dance floor, hoping to locate David in the mob of students. When I finally found him, however, he told me there were more girls he needed to dance with and he would be back later.

During the rest of the night, I sat around, waiting for David to come back and dance with me, or at least check on me. He never did. Even worse, on the ride home he bragged about all the girls he danced with, not even asking how I had enjoyed the evening. As I tried to hold back the tears, I made up my mind right then and there that I never wanted to talk to him again.

The next day I went to my small Bible-study group for girls. That week the study was on communication. We discussed how if you're not willing to confront somebody that hurt you about how you feel, the problem might never be solved and the relationship could be ruined. Immediately I felt the Holy Spirit convicting my heart. I wanted to hold on to my grudge, but I knew that I couldn't.

After the study I marched right on over to David's house. I found him sitting in the basement strumming his guitar.

"David, I was hurt that you ditched me at the dance. I felt like you didn't care about me," I said. "But I shouldn't have been so angry and unforgiving. Can you forgive me?"

Taken back, he set his guitar down.

"Sure," he answered. "And sorry about last night. I...I should have been more thoughtful."

That day I walked home glad that even though nothing will change what happened, at least we did not let it get in the way of our relationship. And all because of a little communication and forgiveness.

Day 7

Felix J., age 18

Do to others as you would have them do to you.

Luke 6:31

I enjoy taking road trips; the premature death of my last car is excellent evidence of this. The actual driving is usually uneventful and rather relaxing, but this was not the case on one summer night. I had gone to Winchester, Virginia, about an hour and a half from my hometown to attend a party with some friends. Around midnight, I left the party alone for the long haul back home. Along a rural road near the interstate, I noticed two Arab-American men pushing a red pickup truck with its flashers on. I slowed down and asked them if they needed help, hoping that they would just need to use my cell phone or something equally quick and painless. After all, I was quite tired at this point and didn't feel up to doing any manual labor, like helping push the truck. The man on the driver's side of the truck (who later introduced himself as Muhammad) asked if I could take him to the nearest gas station, which was about ten

25

miles from where we were. I hesitated a bit, considering the wisdom of "don't pick up strangers," a phrase that all teenage drivers get brainwashed with at some point. But, despite my worries, I offered the men a ride. Muhammad agreed to go, but his friend (who never introduced himself) opted to stay with the truck, probably because my car had no backseats.

Once Muhammad and I arrived at the gas station, he got out to pump the gas into a small container while I sat in the car and listened to music, ever so slightly paranoid that he did have malicious intentions. I realized after about five minutes that I didn't smell any gas. It seemed that Muhammad had never really used a gas pump before, so I had to start the flow for him and chose "premium" grade at his insistence. I loaned him a dollar to pay the bill and took him back to his unnamed friend, who was taking a nap in the truck bed when we returned. After making sure that the truck started, Muhammad pulled a large bundle of cash from behind his seat and offered it to me. I surely could have used the money, but I refused. I left them with one of my business cards as a friendly gesture, and bid them farewell.

I later shared this story with my mom, who rambled for hours about how I was insane, they could've been criminals, I could've ended up dead, etc., etc. Admittedly, the man could very easily have harmed me, leaving me hours from home with no one around. But he didn't, and I made it home safely.

I always try to stop to help a motorist who appears to be in need, because I would want people to do that for me. The Golden Rule is so often ignored in our society, except when a person will be rewarded for his or her efforts.

While it is realistic to fear those who might try to deceive us, the prospect of bringing joy to another person outweighs the risk of being hurt in my mind.

DAY 8

DAVID, AGE 27

Therefore I tell you, do not worry about your life, what you will eat or drink; or about your body, what you will wear. Is not life more important than food, and the body more important than clothes…but seek first His kingdom and His righteousness, and all these things will be given to you as well.

Matthew 6:25, 33

When I was eleven years old, the entire sixth-grade class of Fairbrook Elementary School was bussed off to a nearby nature preserve called Glen Helen for a weeklong overnight nature camp and educational experience. That was the first time I'd spent that much time away from home. It was also the first time I met Buzz.

Buzz was the ugliest creature I'd ever seen. He was a turkey vulture—a giant beast of a bird whose wingspan was easily five or six feet. He had a gathering of red and black loose skin around his head, like a deformed turkey. His feathers were oily and black, and he gripped the board he was sitting on with hideous, pink feet punctuated by yellowed talons.

Even the most adventurous boys, the ones who willingly ran to hold the snakes or touch the toads, didn't want to get anywhere near the thing.

As I look back on it, I realize that what we all felt around that cage was both fear and pity—as though we were looking at a sad, caged monster. I suppose, in a sense, we were. A few years before, some rangers had found an abandoned turkey vulture nest. The egg was hatched in the bird nursery, and the bird—this rare species—was raised in captivity. When the time came to release it into the wild, the rangers took Buzz to a ledge overlooking a small canyon. But Buzz never left his perch. Confused, he just sat there. Thousands of acres open to him. But he turned around and went back into his cage for some chipped mouse meat.

He hasn't left since.

That image of Buzz, choosing to hobble back into his flimsy prison instead of soaring majestically to freedom, continues to haunt me. It haunts me because I'm the same way. How often do I start the day giving only a cursory thought to the Lord? How often do I go through the day entirely unaware and uninterested in the adventure He has for me because I have errands to run? How often do I settle for second best with Jesus because I am distracted by the petty issues of everyday life?

Every day I have to remind myself what I have at my fingertips because of what Christ has done. Everyday, I have to remind myself not to be like Buzz.

DAY 9

SEAN, AGE 24

For I consider that our present sufferings are not worth comparing with the glory that will be revealed in us.

Romans 8:18

I was born with a rare bone condition called osteogenesis imperfecta. This condition causes the bones to be extremely fragile and stunted in growth. Both my childhood and teenage years were filled with pain. By the time I turned eighteen years of age, I had experienced over two hundred bone fractures. Something as simple as sneezing could snap a collarbone or a few ribs. While my friends were outside running and screaming for joy, I was often inside screaming in pain. As the years passed, I watched as my classmates grew taller, but I never did. God kept my soul in a package that could never exceed three feet tall. I often struggled with God as I felt He was unjust for placing me in so much pain, for what appeared to be no reason. That struggle ceased when I was in fourth grade and my excruciating pain collided with divinity.

It was Halloween morning and I was playing around in my living room when all of a sudden I snagged my Halloween costume on the corner of the door. The snag snapped my right femur from the impact. I was furious. Not because I knew I had several weeks of healing ahead of me; rather I knew I was going to miss the Halloween party and trick-or-treating. I felt like God was way out of line this time. I felt He was punishing me for no reason. While holding my right leg in excruciating pain I cried out, "Why me, God? What did I ever do to deserve this? I am just a little boy."

My mother came racing in the room and ran her fingers through my hair to calm me down. This happened so often that there was nothing she could do but keep my body immobilized and distract my mind from the pain. When she realized that my pain coupled with my anger was torture, she centered herself and then proceeded to do something extremely profound. She gently posed a question.

"Sean, is this physical condition going to be a gift or a burden in your life?" As I lay on the floor clenching my fists in agony, it took me two seconds to answer that question. In the first second I thought to myself that this woman must be out of her mind. A gift is something that comes wrapped in a package and placed under a Christmas tree. This was no gift. Then I felt this warm wind swirl around my me. The presence of Christ cloaked my body and the answer became apparent. I was experiencing something everyone alive experiences...pain! We all have pain, how we deal with our pain makes all the difference. I realized I could empathize with people in pain and that I had something in common with everyone.

I looked into my mother's eyes and said, "You're right, Mom; this is a gift." After I moved past self-pity, the course of my life changed forever. I began accomplishing things most people have never dreamed of. I have traveled to forty-five states and five countries, worked in the White House with the president of the United States, and authored my first book by the age of twenty. I am proud God has helped me to triumph over my challenges.

DAY 10

DAN, AGE 21

And we know that in all things God works for the good of those who love him, who have been called according to his purpose.

Romans 8:28

I have never been a big fan of change; maybe that is why the thought of moving halfway through my high-school career scared me. I was a sophomore in high school in Annapolis, Maryland, when my dad accepted a job offer to work for a major company headquartered in Fort Lauderdale, Florida. While my dad was excited about the job change and the opportunity to advance his career while working on Florida's east coast, I was less than thrilled at the idea of moving. I would have to start over in a different city and high school where everyone was a stranger!

I had worked so hard to develop strong friendships in Annapolis, and to succeed socially and academically in high school; the idea of giving up my success in both areas did not sit well with me. I was set to become a captain on the varsity basketball team and to play varsity lacrosse, and I did not want to be forced to struggle making these teams at a new school in Florida. I did not want to leave Annapolis for Florida, period. I was really hurting inside at the idea of moving because I was convinced that my parents didn't really care about how the move affected me or what I thought about moving. I became extremely short-tempered with my parents; I lashed out at them constantly. "Why don't you care about what I think?!"

I feared the move was a done deal, until one day when my parents and I finally discussed my feelings about the situation. I was calm, honest, and upfront with them because it really seemed like they were listening to me. It was much easier than I expected.

"Your dad and I have really noticed how opposed to our move you are, and we were wondering what alternatives you might suggest," my mom said.

"I know that Dad has to take this new job, but is there anyway I can stay in Annapolis, and not move?" I replied, stuttering. I didn't think they would take me seriously, but it was worth a try.

We decided to pray about the decision, and seek God's guidance. I was amazed at how seriously my parents listened to my concerns about moving. I was also surprised when they started talking with me about alternatives to moving. We began talking with different families in the Annapolis area about the possibility of me living with them for my two remaining years of high school. My parents and I agreed that we felt God leading us to the decision for me to remain in Annapolis to complete my high-school career while my parents, brother, and sister, all moved to Florida. "We love you so much, and we want the best for you, even if it's not easy for me and your mom," my dad told me right before they left for Florida.

Although it was extremely hard to watch the rest of my family move to Florida without me—and I am sure it was even much harder for my parents to watch me stay behind—I was happy to remain in Annapolis and confident that we were following God's will. I ended up living with my basketball coach's family for my last two years of high school, and my family ended up moving back to Annapolis directly following my high-school graduation.

When my parents first mentioned the move, I assumed that my destiny was exile in Florida, so I lashed out at my parents. My parents proved, though, that they do care about what I think. They loved me enough to allow me to stay in Annapolis, as difficult as it was. To me, it seemed like nothing good could ever come from the idea of moving. But God used it for good in my relationship with my parents. God always knows what He's doing, even when I don't.

Day 11

JOSH, AGE 19

From everyone who has been given much, much will be demanded.
Luke 12:48

Having one leg is a bit like being a celebrity. If you ever meet a celebrity, ask them about whatever it was that made them famous and watch their eyes glaze over as they recite their answer for the millionth time. Likewise, ask someone with one leg about their disability and you can bet you're hearing a canned answer they've given for years.

I've never actually been a celebrity, but I do have some experience having one leg. Ten years, to be exact. In that time I've been blessed to see God use my story about losing my leg to cancer and eventually becoming a nationally ranked ski racer to encourage thousands through my motivational speeches.

Sometimes it's fun to talk about having one leg. I'd love to tell you about how I can't be killed by lighting because my body doesn't form a circuit with the ground, or about how much time I save only tying one shoe. But for the most part, I'm bored with it. Not bitter—just bored.

In fact, when it came to writing a devotional for this book, the last thing I wanted to talk about was having one leg. But then my mind wandered through Bible stories I've heard since I was a small boy. I thought, for example, about the blind man Jesus healed by spitting in the dirt and then applying the mixture to his eyes.

At first I'm sure this man wanted to tell everyone about the miracle. But after a few years and a few thousand retellings, he probably started to get bored with the story. He would be out swapping stories on the back deck of his apartment in downtown Jerusalem when one of his buddies would turn to him and say, "Hey dude, tell us the one about Jesus spitting in your eyes again!"

"No, you idiot!" someone else would interrupt. "He spit on the *ground*. By the way, what did that mud feel like? Was it crunchy or creamy?"

And for the thousandth time he'd recite the story—the darkness, the warmth on his eyelids, the blinking, the bright light. Word for word, he knew that story through and through.

But you know what? I bet every time he told it, every single time, no matter how bored he felt, his audience sat still on the edge of their seats. The listeners shuddered every time he mentioned the mud in his eyes, and when he talked about his first sight—Jesus standing in front of him, grinning ear to ear—they burst into applause.

"Praise God!" they shouted.

It doesn't matter if the story has been told a million times or not even once—God can use it. Whether it's a story about blindness or cancer or even God's perfect provision in everyday life, He has given every single Christian a story, and no matter how boring or even painful it is to tell, God wants to use it. He's just waiting for you to share.

Day 12

Webb, age 19

The one who received the seed that fell among the thorns is the man who hears the word, but the worries of this life and the deceitfulness of wealth choke it, making it unfruitful. But the one who received the seed that fell on good soil is the man who hears the word and understands it. He produces a crop, yielding a hundred, sixty or thirty times what was sown.

Matthew 13:22-23

It's hard to pinpoint an exact moment when my worries went over the top. At first they came from leading a Bible study, but then they moved to my college housing problems and a huge paper I had procrastinated on for weeks.

Whatever that final straw was, it took me from a servant's heart into the meanest of grouches. I was pacing around my dorm room trying to figure out what to write in my paper when I just couldn't take it anymore. I dropped all my notes on the floor and stormed out of the room.

After downing two Whoppers at Burger King I was back at my desk attempting to start working on the paper.

Just then my unsaved roommate John walked into the room. Although normally I would've tried to be a loving friend to him, today I found myself uninterested in witnessing or even talking to him. I was too stressed, too worried.

For the next several hours I just stared at the wall and thought about how stressed I was. Not only was I starting to question God's plan in my life, I started wondering how there could be a God of love who could take me from a spiritual high to a spiritual low almost instantaneously. Then my eye caught my Bible on the corner of the desk. I picked it up and God brought me to Matthew chapter thirteen where Jesus tells the parable about the farmer who plants seeds in his field. I'd heard the story a hundred times, but on this night as I read the parable, something struck me: I was like the seed that had fallen among the thorns. Sitting there at my desk I knew Jesus was telling me that Satan had brought his thorns of worries and was trying to take my focus off of God's plan of worshipping and serving Him.

Since that night I have been challenging myself to hand my worries to Christ, and I can definitely say that my stress level has been much lower. It's like God has become my weed whacker, cutting down everything that used to worry me! Even better than that, although I sometimes wonder what God is doing in the short term, the mountains I've seen moved as time passes have been amazing!

One example where my attitude has changed is in witnessing to John. Early on in the year I found myself so worried about saying the right words to him that I was freaked out I was going to mess up. God has totally taken that worry from me and shown how He is in control and has an awesome plan.

As Christians, we are all seeds and my prayer is that we won't be choked out by the worries of this life, but instead fall on good soil and yield a crop thirty, sixty, or even one hundred times what was sown.

DAY 13

JOSH, AGE 20

'For I know the plans I have for you', declares the Lord, 'plans to prosper you, and not to harm you, plans to give you hope and a future.'

Jeremiah 29:11

A few years ago my family made up its mind to move. Our house, we decided, had become too small, and the neighborhood was becoming unfriendly. One neighbor would shoot fireworks at one in the morning and their debris would end up in our pool. We only had one bathroom and my little sister was getting into the "make-up process"—we needed at least one more bathroom! After weeks of prayer, we put our house on the market. Two days later, it sold for full asking price. Some people wait years to sell their house! That was a clear answer to prayer, but where were we going to live? We had not found a house yet! We continued to pray and the next week we found a house out in the so-called "boonies." The house was much bigger and much more isolated, which we wanted. God blessed us with a few acres of land and a house big enough to entertain groups of family and friends. We've had several parties for birthdays and had great times of fellowship. The bigger yard has given my dad and I an excuse to work together, talk together. It's funny how much a change in environment can help relationships.

A few years after we moved, God again demonstrated the power of taking a leap of faith. Just before graduation, I felt a tug on my heart to break up with Julie, a girl I had been seeing for almost a year. We painfully agreed it was the best thing to do; she and I would be so far away for college and for the summer, and the distance would have made things impossible. We were best friends and spent so much time together. Our relationship was founded on Christ and we prayed together and really had a great relationship, but for now, Christ needed all my time. That summer, I worked as a camp counselor at Grace Bible Camp. If I had still been dating Julie, I would not have been able to focus all my attention on becoming friends with my campers or becoming closer to Christ. I needed to set a good example for my campers and allow them to see Christ in me. He allowed me to learn things about Himself I had never thought about before, because now my mind was not focusing on another person. It allowed me to put my full focus on Christ and truly study His Word and allow His hand to guide me. Emotionally, it was a hard decision—it's still difficult to talk to her—but I know it was for the best.

Now I'm a college student, just like millions of college students throughout the world. I don't know what I will be doing in twenty years or even next week, but God does. God is full of promises. His Word carries more promises and plans than our human minds can fathom. Plans that are going to help us along and not hurt us, plans to give us hope and an abundant life full of joy. We face complicated decisions constantly; sometimes it feels like God's answer—God's plan—just makes things harder. But in the long run, it doesn't. God's plans, though sometimes difficult to follow, always work out for the best. Take a leap of faith; you've nowhere to fall but His arms.

DAY 14

JIM, AGE 17

Not only so, but we also rejoice in our sufferings, because we know that suffering produces perseverance; perseverance, character; and character, hope.

Romans 5:3-4

My family is very much accustomed to going to our lake house during the summer to enjoy (or maybe to disrupt?) the peace and quiet. We go every summer and enjoy the hot sun while skiing, wakeboarding, tubing, and playing games. To get there, we must voyage three hours south on the highway as one big family. Granted, three hours doesn't sound like a lot, but pack six people into a van, and things can get pretty hectic from time to time.

On one not-so-special trip home, we happened to slide through town to drop off a video—a normal event for the family. But across the parking lot a vending machine advertising thirty-five-cent sodas caught our eye, and of course we had to rake in on those. Since I was tucked away in the car, my mom bought me a Sprite and passed it back to me.

So what did I do? Naturally and instinctively I opened it, but in retrospect, instinct wasn't a good choice in this particular situation. My soda fizzed loudly, exploded, and ended up saturating my pants from top to bottom. My next instinct was to flip out and throw a fit—I had to ride three hours with six people and sticky pants!—but this instinct I was able to overcome. I wasn't very happy at first, but when I thought about the situation a little bit, I realized it wasn't a big deal, but only a miniscule bit of suffering. Even thought I was a little bit sticky, I laughed it off and was able to regain my smile and enjoy the rest of the trip home quite a lot.

Now I know this isn't exactly the worst suffering I've experienced in life, and in fact, it may be the easiest of them all. But really, we will all only have a few big, huge, life-changing tragedies during our time on Earth. Most of the time our difficulty in life is going to be the sum total of lots of little events—soda spilled on the pants, a traffic jam when you're running late, rain on the day of the big game, stuff like that. But learning how to cope with the little things helps to build the perseverance we'll need when coping with the big, life-changing things. If we can't be like Christ in the spilled sodas of life, how can we ever expect to be like Christ when it's really difficult? In the end, it's how we respond to these little events that makes all the difference.

Kristina,
Your story is awesome!
I know God is going to
use it powerfully all over
the world.
R Bradly
Psalm 9:9-10

DAY 15

KRISTINA, AGE 17 → 18

*You are the light of the world. A city on a hill cannot be hidden…
In the same way, let your light shine before men, that they may see
your good deeds and praise your Father in heaven.*

Matthew 5:14, 16

I was driving home late one night soon after I had gotten
my license. It was dark and foggy, so visibility wasn't too
great (meaning I couldn't see much in front, behind, or on
either side of my car). My sister was asleep in the passenger
seat, and I had the radio turned up just loud enough to
keep me awake, but not loud enough to disturb her.

As I came up over a hill, still about ten minutes from
home, I saw a light flash across the sky. Just as quickly as it
appeared, it was gone. I thought it was lightening, but I
wasn't hearing any thunder, so it had to be something else.
A few seconds later, it flashed again, and then again. By
now, I was really confused; I was trying to figure out what
this light was and why it was flashing across the sky in
seemingly random intervals. The light flashed again.

47

I was still driving, still trying to make sense of this mystery, when a sign by the side of the road caught my eye. The sign said "AIRPORT" and had an arrow pointing down a side road to the left. Once again the light flashed. This time, though, I was finally able to make sense of it. This wasn't just any old light flashing across the sky for no apparent reason. This light was a special beacon from the airport, lighting up the night sky to show airplane pilots where to land.

As I drove the rest of the way home, I continued to think about that light flashing across the sky. When we got home, I tried to tell my sister about the light, but before I could, she mumbled something about "quiet" and "sleep" and shut her bedroom door. For some reason, though, I couldn't stop thinking about the airport beacon lighting up the night sky. As I was trying (rather unsuccessfully) to get to sleep, the above verses from Matthew chapter five came into my mind.

I realized that when Jesus was talking about us being "the light of the world," He didn't mean that we were supposed to shine like almost burnt-out flashlight bulbs. No, He meant for us to light up this dark world like the light from that airport had lit up the whole night sky. In the same way that the light I saw was meant to show pilots the way to safety and warn them of danger, we are supposed to "shine before men," showing them the way to the Father in Heaven.

I want to make sure that I am living my life so passionately for Christ that people can't help but notice. I started checking my light every now and then just to be sure that it's still burning brightly. I want to make sure that I'm talking about Christ, following His teachings, and practicing what I preach. Will you join me in my attempts to "let my light shine before men"?

DAY 16

MARK, AGE 32

But the LORD said to Samuel, "Do not consider his appearance or his height, for I have rejected him. The LORD does not look at the things man looks at. Man looks at the outward appearance, but the LORD looks at the heart."

1 Samuel 16:7

The Baptist church where I came to know the Lord had a church member who was a retired minister. He would faithfully give a hearty "amen" to every single song special or drama regardless of how wonderfully or terribly it was delivered. People (often youth group members) crawled up on the altar platform and died to themselves to give their best for God. By most measurements of talent, many of these performances were terrible, but the "amen" was given for their enthusiasm for God, not technical performance.

After I had been a Christian for some time I was invited to share my testimony in a small church in the rural Virginia countryside. The church worship team had an unusual configuration of musicians that included several guitar players. During worship each instrument was obviously out of tune and everyone was off beat. It was probably the worst-sounding live music that I've ever heard. But the team and congregation were worshiping wholeheartedly out of sincere gratitude to God. I don't recall seeing even one face in the church grimacing with pain due to the bad music. They were caught up in the object—not the quality—of the worship.

Years later I went to the Biblical Art Museum in Dallas, Texas. As we toured through a solo artist's exhibition I commented how crude and poor I thought most of his works were. Almost immediately a man with a mild disability walked up and introduced himself as the artist. He shared his powerful testimony and vision and I was completely humbled. I was using worldly lenses to judge his art.

Through these three experiences God has taught me a powerful lesson. We live in an age of real-time voice-pitch correction, computer-enhanced photos, plastic surgery, teeth whitening, etc. Cultural things like primetime-television talent competitions, which humiliate or eliminate anyone whose performance is less than perfect, also affect our mindset towards others. But Scriptures like 1 Samuel 16:7 remind me the world's standard is outward perfection, but the Lord looks at the heart—and so should I.

DAY 17

MICAELA, AGE 18

You will not fear the terror of night, nor the arrow that flies by day, nor the pestilence that stalks in the darkness, nor the plague that destroys at midday.

Psalm 91:5-6

I recently went on a trip with my friend to Spain and France. While packing, mere hours before leaving for the airport, it hit me: I was going over three thousand miles away from my home, family and friends. Karen was already in Spain; I was supposed to fly over by myself and meet her. How was I supposed to do this on my own? Brushing my doubts aside, I finished zipping up my suitcase. Out of the corner of my eye, I noticed a card from my uncle. In it was Psalm 91. I skimmed it quickly and went back to packing so we could get to the airport.

Later, while sitting at the airport with my family, I was overcome by the fear that I would never see them again and would meet my untimely death in an alley in Spain. I almost didn't want to go to Spain—I just wanted to sit in my room and hang out with my family.

Thankfully, I got over that. I boarded my plane and was off to Spain. The plane ride went smoothly and I made my connecting flight with time to spare. Karen and her family met me when I landed in Madrid, ready to take me to their apartment. That day, I read that just a few days before I left, two young girls had been killed in broad daylight. In my mind, those two girls became my friend and me. The fear did not subside once I settled into the apartment

Every man who walked by me was a suspect, waiting to turn around and kill me. I heard gunshots and covered my head, hoping that they wouldn't ricochet into the house. It took a few minutes to realize no one was trying to kill me; they were merely celebrating the victory of a soccer game by setting off firecrackers. Every person talking on the street was plotting an attack on the apartment and every yelling person was angrily declaring war on the two American girls sleeping upstairs. Even though the apartment was in a small, relatively safe neighborhood, the bars on the windows didn't comfort me. In my experience bars meant one of two things: either they were there to keep me in (which I guessed wasn't the case), or trying to keep death and attack out, which only strengthened my fear.

The first night in Madrid I laid wide-awake, hearing every sound. The people laughing outside, the dogs barking, cars backfiring... Every sound was a murder attempt. In my exhausted, fearful state I crawled out of bed and made my way to my suitcase. Every noise I made seemed deafening; I was sure the murderers could hear me now.

I'm not even sure why I decided to open my suitcase, but inside was a small Bible—the last thing I expected to find. My father had put the Bible inside my suitcase without me realizing it, knowing it would be the greatest travel companion. By the neon lights outside my window, to the laughing and yelling of Spanish, I re-read Psalm 91, more in depth this time. I got back into my bed and said a simple prayer that I barely remember now.

"Dear God, help me to remember that You are with me always and that You will safely lead me back to my home and my family...."

After only a few lines of the prayer I began to feel calm and at peace. I could feel God's presence around me and I knew that God had sent angels to protect me. I couldn't see them, but I could feel that they were there, all around me. From that point on, I wasn't as scared of the bars on the windows, or the men walking by me, or the laughing and yelling in the street. God was there when I needed Him most; He comforted me when I could stand no more fear. Now, every time I get scared I remember that night, when God sent a host of angels to watch me.

DAY 18

JENNIFER, AGE 15, AUSTRALIA

For you created my inmost being; you knit me together in my mother's womb. I praise you because I am fearfully and wonderfully made; your works are wonderful, I know that full well.

Psalm 139:13-14

I knew I was born in South Korea, but when I found out the whole story of my adoption and my background, my heart felt like it had burst into a zillion pieces. I felt like I was having an identity crisis. I didn't know who I really was and wondered if I was worth anything.

I remember sitting at the kitchen table one afternoon when my mum and I got on to the subject of adoption. My parents had told me about it when I was younger but now, being older, I wanted to know more, so I asked her, "Hey Mum, what can you tell me about my biological parents?" thinking that this would satisfy some of my curiosity about them.

To my disappointment, what my mum told me was far from a skip down memory lane—it left me crying, extremely confused, and really cut. I found out that my biological parents had broken up before I was born. I had assumed that my mum's boyfriend walked out on her, leaving her to look after me, so I had this hate towards my father. But, in fact, she never even knew she was pregnant before they broke up. So then, I felt like I was unplanned and was a mistake and I had bitterness towards my mother as well. I didn't know who to hate.

I was so lost in my emotions. In my mind this voice said to me, "See, you weren't planned." It kept going, saying, "And look, she wasn't married. You're the product of something sinful." And at that, I was so ashamed and bruised that I believed every word and clung onto any hate that I could. I thought I was nothing.

The grudges grew bigger through that year until the Holy Spirit knocked me on the noggin and told me to "talk to God and give all of your pain to Him." I didn't want to, but I knew He wanted me to. When I did, He told me that I needed to forgive my biological father and mother. I admit, forgiving them wasn't easy, but I know now that it was the best choice I've made as a person and as a Christian.

The coolest thing is, I look back now and I see the facts, that, yeah, my past wasn't perfect, but I know the truth is I am fearfully and wonderfully made and God loves me. He had an awesome plan all mapped out for me before I was even born. I wasn't a mistake. Our Creator planned me.

Confessing my hurts to God and letting Him do the healing work rather than me, set me free from my emotional burdens—and also helped me grow as a Christian in a stronger way.

We are fearfully and wonderfully made! He made us and thinks we are so incredibly awesome and extremely good-looking!

In the end, I've found His works are wonderful; after all, I am one of them...now I know that full well.

DAY 19

KATHRYN, AGE 16

Let the wise listen and add to their learning, and let the discerning get guidance.

Proverbs 1:5

When I was about fourteen, I was very focused on having fun and being a kid, never really thinking about listening to God, or even talking to Him. I thought going to church and praying was enough to be a good Christian. I did what my parents told me; I was a good kid. Life was great.

Everything changed when my family and I went camping with our church small group at Highland Retreat. Highland was a familiar place for me; our church used the campground and retreat center on a regular basis for our events. Still, there was something special about Highland; time doesn't seem to pass there. It's a place where there are no worries. I always loved to go and just sit beside the creek to listen to the sounds of the forest, feel the breeze in my hair.

On this particular day there was no one around. There were none of the normal kids hunting for crayfish or minnows, no one was even riding past it on their bikes. It was a perfect opportunity to be alone, away from everyone.

I sat in my usual spot on the bridge, with my feet dangling over the water. I listened to the sound of the water rushing past the rocks, the birds singing to each other in the trees. I watched the little fish and tadpoles dash around in the creek. While I was sitting, it dawned on me that every single thing I heard and watched and felt, God had created with infinite care and attention to detail. As I sat in awe, I felt a sudden urge to talk to God, not only to talk but also to listen. For at least thirty minutes, I sat listening to God and telling Him everything I was feeling. It was that day, listening and talking to God, that I realized I needed not only to go to church and believe in God, but to have a relationship with Him.

I had asked God to live in my heart and walk with me through my life journey before, but when I asked him to come and live in my heart that day I felt like He answered loudly. "Yes!" I was ready. I truly understood what it meant to accept Christ.

Since that day, God has never felt far away. He has always been walking with me or carrying me through my life journey. I was baptized the following summer and I still make time to talk *and* listen to God, trying to hear what He has to say and what His plans are for my life. God reveals himself in even the subtleties. Instead of going out and looking for God, sit down and listen. It's only a short time before He'll call your name.

DAY 20

KATIE, AGE 22

I delight greatly in the LORD;
my soul rejoices in my God.
For he has clothed me with garments of salvation
and arrayed me in a robe of righteousness,
as a bridegroom adorns his head like a priest,
and as a bride adorns herself with her jewels.

Isaiah 61:10

I remember watching the baptism of a child in my church one Sunday morning when I was fourteen, and listening to the pastor pray, "May this child never remember a time when he did not know and love the Lord." I thought, *Why is that supposed to be a good thing? Doesn't that doom you to complacency?* After all, that's what I thought the problem was for me. I had no exciting testimony, no dramatic conversion experience. Being a Christian was easy for me; I had never been ridiculed for my faith, nor had I seriously doubted what I believed. I figured this was why my relationship with Christ lacked the passion and vigor that I had seen in some of my friends' walks or heard about at youth conferences.

But the real problem had nothing to do with the lack of drama in my life. The problem was my view of myself. I was basically a good kid, so I did not really believe I deserved the same punishment as a convicted rapist or a drug dealer or even kids who made more obvious mistakes than I did. I knew I was sinful, and that I needed God's forgiveness for my sins, but I just didn't think I was "that bad."

At my mother's suggestion, I began reading Jerry Bridge's *Discipline of Grace*. The title of his third chapter, "Preach the Gospel to Yourself," completely baffled me. I was already saved, so why I would need to hear the Gospel again? Soon God showed me why: I had never fully understood how significant it was in the first place! You see, I learned that the Scriptures tell us that God makes no distinction among sinners. This meant that although I may have been a good kid, my sins are no less condemning than those of the most hardened criminal.

Once I grasped my own depravity, the contrasting perfection of Jesus Christ was blindingly obvious. He was willing to give up His throne to live a mortal life and die a most humiliating death to save an ungrateful wretch like me. With such a miraculous foundation, how could my faith ever be dull?

A passionate relationship with Christ does not come from a road-to-Damascus conversion or a completely altered lifestyle. Those can be the fruit of God's work in your life. The joy of the Lord comes from understanding what the Gospel of Jesus Christ means for your life on a daily basis and from wanting to understand its implications more each new morning. How do you do this? By preaching the Gospel to yourself everyday. Believe me, I know how easy it is to gloss over the story of Christ's death and resurrection because you have "heard it a hundred times." But if that's what you are saying, you should probably listen to it again, because therein lies the secret of joy and growth in the Christian life.

DAY 21

MATT, AGE 16

Teach us to number our days.

Psalm 90:12

I'm sure you've had the experience. At some point during the middle of the night, the power cuts off. Everything in your house loses electricity, including your alarm clock. So what happens? Nothing. Your alarm clock turns off and doesn't ring to wake you up. Let me tell you about a morning that and many more things happened to me.

It all started when my Dad came in yelling and waving his arms to let me know I was already fifteen minutes late waking up and that there was no power in the house. This is not the best way to start off a day. So I jumped out of bed and grabbed a fresh pair of boxers from my dresser. Remembering that it would be dark in the bathroom, I brought in a flashlight and left the door open to let in a little light.

I turned on the shower, waited a second for it to warm up, and jumped in. But I quickly discovered that the light from the door was not enough to even find the soap. *Good thinking on bringing the flashlight*, I told myself as I turned it on and carefully positioned it on top of the shower curtain. I was barely lathered up when I heard the most annoying sound in the world. This sound was that of a smoke alarm going off outside the open door of my bathroom because of all the steam let off by my shower.

My mom then came and started yelling about a fire or something, but soon she figured out that it was just the steam, so she switched to yelling to hurry up. Following that she shut the door just hard enough to knock my flashlight off its perch. It made a rapid drop directly onto my head and onto the ground, where it cut off.

So there I was. The smoke alarm was ringing, my mom was yelling, I was running late, there was a bump forming on my head, it was pitch black, I couldn't find the soap, and to top it all off, I was naked.

At that point I was tempted to give up on the day and go back to bed. But then, somewhere between the screeching alarm and the incessant yells from my mom, I started to smile, and then even chuckle. I realized that God has only given us a set number of days, and each one of them is golden, no matter how it starts. So I decided that electricity or no electricity, I would live that day to its fullest potential.

DAY 22

LAURA, AGE 17

For God did not give us the spirit of timidity, but a spirit of power, of love and of self discipline.

2 Timothy 1:7

One of our group leaders, Dave, was going on and on about bungee jumping. Honestly, I thought he was crazy. After all, we were on a bridge standing over Victoria Falls, one of the seven natural wonders of the world, on the border between Zimbabwe and Zambia. It was an unfamiliar country, an unfamiliar language, an unfamiliar culture. We didn't know the people running it, and nobody we knew had done it. How could we be sure it was safe? How could we know that these people were properly trained, or even physically able to operate this? How could we know it was a safe bungee cord? Africa is known to be a poorer continent—could these tourist traps afford proper equipment? The risks obviously outweighed the benefits.

But Dave was just as obviously unaffected by any of the risks. To my horror, I watched him march across the bridge, pay fifty U.S. dollars, and start stepping into his harness. He hobbled across the platform, and prepared himself.

"Five...four...three...two...one...BUNGEE!" Everyone, myself included, counted down to his demise.

He proved me wrong, though. I watched Dave fall 111 meters down towards the base of Victoria Falls with my jaw hanging wide open, watched him bounce, then watched him ride back up to his safety. Not a scratch on his head. Even still, I wasn't convinced that this bungee jumping was a good idea. Just because you come back alive the first time doesn't guarantee that you will the second time as well!

But as I thought about Dave, I realized that bungee jumping was much more than just a little thrill with colossal risks. It was symbolic of his larger walk with Christ. From watching his spiritual life, I've learned that sometimes you just have to take the dive and put your life in someone else's hands.

The Christian faith is one of the biggest leaps we can make. We're supposed to walk and talk and listen with a God that we can't touch, see, or smell. But if we don't make that leap, we'll never be able to experience the joyride of a relationship with our Creator, one that goes not down, but straight up.

When Dave got back to our group, he was raving about his thrilling experience. As students, we weren't allowed to jump, but now I almost (but not quite) wanted to. I wanted to make a leap here, to remind me to make the biggest leap every day for the rest of my life: the leap into God's arms.

DAY 23

REBEKAH, AGE 20

Be still and know that I am God.

Psalm 46:10

Over three years ago, the Lord called my best friend home. His official title was "Dad," but he was more than my dad. He was my teacher, mentor, and above all, best friend. Dad was a godly man of integrity, but he was also fun to be around. He was every daughter's dream. I will forever be grateful to the Lord for blessing me with him. One thing about Dad was that he was constantly planting seeds of wisdom in my heart. Now I remember these conversations in little clips and phrases.

"Daddy, what's it like to feel the Father's pleasure?"

"It's like warm sun on the back of your neck on a cold day," he replied, the light of Jesus beaming from his eyes.

Dad made it a priority to spend time imparting the Word of God to me. He could make godly principles out of anything, anywhere. It happened when we were fishing, raking leaves, or just being together. Looking back now, I can see that these moments were not just memories, but times of preparation for the future.

Dad was a strong, healthy forty-nine-year-old. There was no reason to think the Lord would take him any time soon. But then he woke up one morning with an extremely painful headache and high fever. Our last moment together was before the ambulance came. Delirious, he grasped my shirt trying to ask for a pillow. When I gave it to him I said, "I love you," and I knew he understood. At the hospital we were told that he had contracted bacterial meningitis. The next day, I was waiting outside his room when I heard two words that I'll never forget: "He's gone!" I felt like somebody stuck a knife through my heart. Weeping and momentarily in shock, the strong arms of my youth pastor came around me with love and comfort. My healing started right there. A peace that passes all understanding entered me.

Amazingly, I never questioned or got angry with God. It was like all the "seeds" that Daddy planted began to sprout. His impartation of spiritual truths is a big part of what has given me the strength to carry on and to be a strength and encouragement to Mom. Jesus saw our need and has shown Himself faithful to see us through this deep valley. The Lord keeps bringing me back to His Word where I have found comfort, refuge, and strength.

No matter what kind of trial you are going through, I encourage you not to go by feelings, but hold on to the promises of God. Trust Him. Our Father knows best and would never lay more upon you than you can bear. He will renew your strength and see you through whatever storms you face. He did it for me and He'll do it for you.

As much as I love and miss Daddy, I wouldn't bring him back. I would never want to take him away from the Father. I know we'll be together again forever! That's a promise!

DAY 24

CJ, AGE 19

Live such good lives among the pagans that, though they accuse you of doing wrong, they may see your good deeds and glorify God on the day he visits us.

1 Peter 2:12

My friend Sarah and I were looking for an excuse to get off campus on a sunny day in the middle of last semester. So when she suggested that we hop in her car for a road trip, I was quick to follow her to the parking lot.

"Sarah, I like this little Jesus fish on your bumper here," I said as I pointed to the tiny metallic ichthus on her car.

"Yeah, it's not too bad. It was on the car when I bought it. Actually, I kind of wish that I didn't still have it on," she replied as we climbed in the car.

"And why is that?" I asked, wondering why this Christian friend of mine would want to toss away such a powerful symbol.

"Because I don't really look like much of a Christian when I'm flipping off slow drivers in the right lane of the interstate. I'd rather have a skull and crossbones back there if I'm going to act like that."

I sat silenced in the passenger seat for a few moments, thinking about what she had said. Although her statements shocked me a bit, I was at least proud of Sarah for thinking about the consequences of her actions. She knew that people who saw her car from the back would assume that she was a Christian. And if her actions didn't match up to the message she was communicating, then she was in trouble.

How many times do my own actions conflict with my message? I wondered as we drove down the highway. It's probably hard for people to believe the Christian messages I like to share if they hear me laughing at an inappropriate joke or see me cutting in line at the movie theater. If I do those things, then it's probably as hard for other folks to believe that I'm a Christian as it would be if I were flipping them off on the interstate.

Come to think of it, if people know that I'm a Christian, it's kind of like I have a Jesus fish on me all the time. I take it with me pretty much everywhere I go. My friends and family know I am a Christian, my classmates know that I am a Christian, and my co-workers know that I am a Christian. They see the Jesus fish and expect Christian living from me. And if I don't live up to that expectation, then I'm no better than the angry driver on the interstate—I'm just as much of a hypocrite.

After Sarah's lesson I learned that if people see the Jesus fish, if they know that I am a Christian, then I have a calling to purify my life for God. I need to live my life for His glory and do the things that will bring others closer to

Him. So now I find encouragement from God's Word and strive to live a holy life so that all who know me can see what I do and "glorify God on the day He visits us."

DAY 25

BRANDON, AGE 18

Jesus Christ is the same yesterday and today and forever.

Hebrews 13:8

I plopped down on my bed after another long day. It was mid-December and Christmas was approaching, but in the season of joy where we celebrate the birth of our Savior, I was miserable. Never in my life had I felt so distant from God. After all, I had accepted Christ, so nothing should be going wrong. At a youth camp, I experienced the manifest presence of the Holy Spirit in a real, strong way and I had discovered the intimacy that God desires to have with each person who chooses to serve Him—including me. Yet just a few months later, I was alone in my bedroom in a pit of emotional despair. These days I rarely read my Bible and prayer became a daily chore, a duty to be fulfilled. I had failed. How could I have had such a powerful experience with God and then drift away? What must God think of me?

Sadly, I continued living in that same depressing pattern for the rest of the school year, putting trust in my feelings and acting on what I allowed them to tell me instead of trusting God and His plan. I left no time for Him except for the thirty seconds every night just before I fell asleep, when I'd mutter a self-centered, unfocused mass of sentences and call it a prayer. Not what you might call an intimate relationship with the One who died so that I might live. I didn't know then, but life was about to change.

I graduated in June, and soon after, a friend invited me to a youth retreat. It took place at a local campground and retreat center deep in the heart of the woods. That first evening of the retreat, all the youth gathered around a campfire to sing and praise the Lord. Sitting on old stumps and split-log benches around the crackling flames, all the youth sang "The Heart of Worship" and "All in All." As I sang, an overwhelming sense of that peace I knew so well washed over me, and God spoke to me:

"Brandon, look around you. All that you see, I created. Remember that I am in control, and most of all, I love you."

Only then did I realize what I'd been doing all this time. I had been expecting God to make my life cushy and struggle-free, failing to realize that God never promises anyone an easy life. I had allowed my feelings to lead me instead of following his direction.

Most importantly, though, I learned the gift of waiting. God allowed me to experience a time away from him. It was one of the most difficult things I've ever experienced. Yet I know now that just when I think He has deserted me, He will show up somehow and gently remind me that He is the same yesterday, today, and forever, and He will always be in control.

Kristina –
Thank you For your contribution.
I PRay it will bless everyone that picks It
up – KELSEY

DAY 26

Kelsey, age 27

Flee the evil desires of youth, and pursue righteousness, faith, love, and peace, along with those who call on the Lord with a pure heart.

2 Timothy 2:22

Starting at age ten, I lived in Phoenix, Arizona. Even at that early age I was overcome by the powers of peer pressure and the euphoria of drugs and alcohol. As I grew older, the drugs became more powerful and frequent until I was a junkie, in and out of legal trouble. The only thing I cared about was my next high.

This went on until two years ago when I asked Jesus into my heart and gave Him complete control of my addictions. But that is all I let Him have. My heart was still full of the ungodly actions which I had lived with for so long. I would fly off the handle in an instant, with no regard for anyone's feelings. Even the occasional drug deal was not out of the question to make ends meet. I was not living Christlike whatsoever.

As I became more involved in church, and started to study the Bible, I suddenly became aware of the number 222 showing up in my daily life. This number was everywhere! I would drive down the interstate to the neighboring town and see countless signs for exit 222. I would order a sandwich from a local convenience store and my ticket would get a big blue stamp—222. Getting back change, a total for something bought, even my favorite brand of cigarette was on sale for—and you guessed it—$2.22. What did this mean? Was it just a coincidence? Not at all! It was God's way of speaking to me throughout the day, but this wasn't clear until one day when I was studying a Bible I found in my wife's closet. There, at the beginning of II Timothy, in black and white, like a lightning bolt hitting me, was the verse that would change my life. It was II Timothy 2:22.

It was like a huge burden had been lifted off me when I read that scripture. I knew what was being said to me, and it was coming straight from God's Word. I had to hand more than my addictions over to God; I was to hand my life over, *all of it*! I am to flee evil desires of youth (drugs, money, sex, foul language). All evil desires. I am to pursue a righteousness that can only be learned from my Savior, Jesus Christ, and to learn to be faithful, loving, and peaceful with the help of my fellow Christians. I now have a pure heart, a changed heart. He saved even a wretch like me.

DAY 27

BRAD, AGE 19

Love the Lord your God with all your heart and with all your soul and with all your mind and with all your strength. The second is this: 'Love your neighbor as yourself.' There is no commandment greater than these.

Mark 12:30-31

I snuggled closer to my dad as he finished reading the Bible story, a nightly tradition during the first few years of my life. He closed the book, looked directly at me, and asked, "Brad, why did God put you here?" I thought for a minute, my three-year-old brain puzzled by such a difficult question, and I finally said, "I don't know, Daddy." "You're here to live for the glory of God and the benefit of others," he said. Little did I know how long it would take me to discover the deep meaning behind my father's simple words.

Fast forward to the summer after my senior year. I was eighteen years old, a high school graduate. No more bed time stories from dad, no more simple answers to difficult questions. And I was different, too; somewhere along the way I had become selfish. I remember telling someone once, "At this point in my life the only person who matters is me, and if that means making selfish decisions, then so be it." Exact words out of my mouth.

They say everyone changes in college. Well, add me to that statistic. The turning point in my selfish behavior came sometime in February. I was on men's retreat at Virginia Beach. It was too cold to swim, so my good friend Josh and I decided to see if we could walk all the way to the boardwalk (which turned out to be much further away than it appeared). Well, we returned to the beach house some three hours later and my life was on a different course. During that walk, Josh and I were attempting to figure out how we could make an eternal difference with our lives. We came to the conclusion that giving unselfishly in our relationships with other people is really what life is about.

I was horrified. In a matter of hours I realized that my entire outlook on life was completely wrong and that I had to make some drastic changes. When I returned to school I began trying to figure out how I could have compassion for people that I had been distant from so long. It was a two-step process. First, I began praying. I prayed that God would change my outlook on life, and instill in me a compassion for others. Then I began thinking of some practical steps I could take, like calling old friends and spending more time with other students. As a result, people began to become an important part of my life as my selfishness began to slip away. I still have a long way to go, but at least now I'm on the right track.

I now know that my Dad's advice to "live for the glory of God and the benefit of others" wasn't really his advice at all—it's the same thing Jesus said was the greatest commandment. I also know that God has the power to change even the most selfish person.

DAY 28

CHRISTINE, AGE 21

God had planned something better for us.

Hebrews 11:40a

I was pretty sure life would never get any better than this. Two weeks away from being sweet sixteen and I was dating the guy I'd had a crush on for what seemed like years. He was older, athletic, and so cute! He was absolutely perfect for me—my parents even liked him! Within weeks my imagination was practically setting the wedding date and picking out names for our children! Then one night, my perfect little world started crashing down around me.

"I can't date you anymore."

Wait, I couldn't have heard that right. But, no, he said the same thing again. Why was he saying this?

"I don't know. We can't date anymore, but I want us to still be friends"

Friends? Are you kidding me? I'd just been dumped. And he didn't even have a good reason!

In many ways that one night shaped the rest of my high-school experience. Somewhere in the back of my head was the idea that it was my fault. If I could just change myself enough, I could become the person he wanted as a girlfriend and win him back. Maybe if I just lost enough weight, or excelled academically, or was witty or charming or quiet enough… But nothing I did seemed to work at all. I felt like I was a failure. I ended up spending over a year doing close to nothing at all.

So where was God in all this? Sometimes it felt like He was ignoring my prayers completely, but looking back I can see Him gently whispering that I was praying for the wrong thing. I thought I needed a boyfriend to feel loved. Instead, God was pleading for me to see how much He already loved me. He loves me so much that He gave the life of His only Son so that I can know what Heaven's like. And He doesn't think I'm too dumb, or too tall, or too quiet, or too anything! As God slowly started to change my focus away from this one boy, He opened my eyes to so many other wonderful things I could do. I was able to comfort hurting friends around me. I traveled to Mexico to help build homes. I found a spot in a youth praise band.

God wants so much more for me than a date. As I learn to trust His plans and not make my own, I constantly see His perfect love shown in the way He guides and directs every area of my life.

DAY 29

THOMAS, AGE 19

Jesus replied, "I tell you the truth, if you have faith and do not doubt, not only can you do what was done to the fig tree, but also you can say to this mountain, 'Go, throw yourself into the sea,' and it will be done. If you believe, you will receive whatever you ask for in prayer."

Matthew 21:18-22

Choosing the correct college to spend your next four years of life is a daunting task. As I began to consider my choices during high school, all my friends gave me one piece of advice: "Pray about it." So I did. I kept praying and considering my options and then praying some more.

After a while a certain school seemed to feel right when compared to all the others, and it was that school that became my number-one choice. I spent hours going through the process every college-bound high-schooler does: taking SATs, writing essays, and sending out applications. And in my case, praying. Lots of praying.

My heart was racing that day in early December when my mother called me at track practice to tell me to hurry home because an "envelope" was waiting from the school. She handed it to me when I walked through the door. I checked the return address. Sure enough, it read, "The College of William and Mary," my first choice.

Years of hard work rested on whatever was inside. I carefully broke the seal on the envelope and unfolded the letter. My eyes immediately locked onto one word in the first paragraph: "Congratulations"

"Yeah!"

I held the letter above my head in victory.

"I'm in!"

A few weeks later, when all my relatives were gathered at Christmas, my grandmother motioned for me to come stand beside her. "I have been praying for your acceptance to William and Mary every day," she said.

Besides a mumbled thank you, I was left speechless. It had never occurred to me that others could have a hand in praying for my acceptance to school. My acceptance was not only an answer to my prayer, but it was also an answer to her prayer.

Soon Christmas was over and summer had arrived. Now I had a whole new set of things to pray about. Would my roommate be a good one? Would I find good Christian friends? The list went on and on.

Arriving at school, I found that my prayers for a good roommate, strong Christian friends, and everything else were once again answered in ways I would never have dreamed of. I also found that I was an answer to prayers of people at my new school.

Once again, God showed me how He works through the prayers of many different people to accomplish His will. It's like a giant "prayer web" that Christians are called to be a part of. We pray, others pray, and God works in our hearts. I have no doubt that my "it just feels right" description of William and Mary was God all along. He had everything planned for me and I just had to put my faith in Him.

DAY 30

JOSH, AGE 22

Your attitude should be the same as that of Christ Jesus.

Philippians 2:5

Have you ever just had one of those days? Ya know...when things just don't go your way? You wake up, there's no milk for your cereal, you're late for school, you almost get arrested by the FBI. You know, one of those kinds of days.

Several months ago I did almost get arrested by the FBI. True story. I was flying home to California from Kansas. I was in the airport in Kansas going through the security checkpoint, and, as you know, airport security is a much more lengthy and in-depth process, post-9/11.

So, I go through the metal detector area, and then, this gentleman says to me, "Sir, do you mind if we do an additional screening on your bag." I said, "No, go right ahead." So this guy places my carry-on bag up on a table, rubs my bag down with a cloth, sticks the cloth in a machine, and the machine goes, "BEEP!" The beep indicated that my bag had just tested positive for explosives. Not a good thing. So then, the guy asks, "Sir, what do you do for a living?" Ummm, I'm a motivational speaker; I'm just trying to make a difference in the world. And I'm sure he was thinking, *Yeah, sure you are, buddy.*

He then asks if I am carry any explosives or dangerous objects in my bag. "Absolutely not." So he tries again. Rubs bag with cloth, sticks cloth in machine. BEEP! Again it tests positive for explosives. So now he calls over his manager. Manager rubs bag with cloth, sticks cloth in machine. BEEP! Again.

So, then the manager gets on the intercom system and says, "Yeah, we got a situation 543-9'er over." I then glance down the hallway and see a squadron, I mean, an entire platoon of FBI agents walking down the hall. So there's, like, fifteen of these guys.

Meanwhile, they've got me held up in this glass cubicle like I'm Osama bin Laden or something. And I'm nervous. I'm sweating like Mike Tyson at a spelling bee. And then, this elderly woman walks by me and kindly states, "You're sick!"

And I'm like, "I didn't DOOO anything."

So, these fifteen FBI agents circle my bag as if they are about to play ring around the rosey. Then one of them inquires, "Sir, do you mind if we open up your bag?" So of course I say, "Yes, please, go right ahead." (What am I going to say? "No, no, sir, I don't think that'd be a good idea for any of us?") So he begins to open up my bag.

Now, something I should inform you of, is that I often travel with a lot of odd and funny props. So the man opens up my carry-on bag and pulls out a Sponge Bob doll, some fake leaves, and my stuffed dog I call Snoop. About this time, I'm sure he is thinking, *Yep, if he's not a terrorist, then at the very least this guy is psycho.*

So finally, one exhausting hour later, we finally figure out at the place where I had just spoken, they had a fireworks display and some of the smoke and residue had gotten on my bags. So then, they release me and I am relieved, but now I realize that I am running late for my flight. They are holding the plane for me. I'm the last one to get on. Understand, when you are the last person to get on a flight, you are about as welcome as a mosquito at a nudist colony. I see that there is one open seat, and it is mine. I sit down in the aisle seat next to this gentleman, and as I normally do when I sit next to someone, I greet him. Try to picture this. I say, "Hello, how are you?" That's all I say.

Here's how he responds to me. I won't tell you exactly what he said, because, personally, I choose not to use vulgar language. So I will just insert the word BUNNY. Here's what he said. He said, "I want you to rip off my BUNNY head, pull my BUNNY brains out of my BUNNY head, throw my BUNNY brains on the ground, then reattach my BUNNY head to my BUNNY neck!!!"

Wow…okay. I just sat there thinking, *Hey, buddy, don't mess with me, I just tested positive for explosives!* But I didn't say that; instead I said, "Sir, are you feeling okay?" He said, "Yeah I just have a headache." A headache? Is that all? What would he have said if he had the flu?

The point is that I believe in life we don't always choose what happens to us, but we do choose how we react. I would submit to you that the test of a real person's character is how he acts when things are not going so well. It's easy for us to have a positive attitude when things are great, but how do you react when things are not so great?

We should have the same attitude as Jesus: an attitude of unconditional love, unparalleled compassion, and endless mercy. Attitude is contagious—is yours worth catching?

Cassie
Arnold

DAY 31

CASSIE, AGE 13

A father to the fatherless, a defender of widows, is God in His holy dwelling.

Psalm 68:5

My dad could be my next-door neighbor and I would never know. He left my mom before I was born and has never been back. I have never even seen him.

Don't get me wrong. I have been raised in a great family; my mother loves me, and my sister is one of my best friends. But ever since I was little I have always wanted a daddy. In fact, I grew to hate my father for all the pain and tears he had caused me. I knew that he didn't love me and that was the hardest part.

My heart broke when I looked at my mom's divorce certificate, because it said "no children were born to the marriage." Knowing that my father refused to even admit that he had a child tore me apart. Every time I used to think of my dad, tears would come to my eyes and my heart would well up with anger. But something happened three years ago that changed everything.

I went to Toronto, Canada, because I heard about the revival that was going on up there. The Spirit of God was there, and I was slain in the spirit. As the power of God came on me, all strength left my body and I fell on the floor. While I was on the ground, a woman kneeled beside me and spoke a word over me that totally rocked my world. This woman did not even know me, but she said, "Some people can say that their father is a movie star or the president of the United States, but you can say that your father is the creator of the universe." Even though there were thousands of other people there, I felt like I was the only one in the room. God touched my heart and left His fingerprint that night. I realized that God really did love me, and that I wanted to live that love.

I had never thought of God in that way before. I now have strength in knowing that I will never be without a daddy, and that is a miracle as far as I am concerned. I'm not saying that I now love my earthly father and want to contact him, because I don't, but I am able to pray for him now. It is still hard, and I still deal with this issue every single day. The big difference is that I don't have to face this alone anymore. Now when I pray I don't say, "Dear God." I say, "Daddy!" I praise God for the work that He has done in my heart.

I can finally say that I am a daddy's girl.

DAY 32

BRIAN, AGE 18

Therefore do not worry about tomorrow, for tomorrow will worry about itself.

Matthew 6:34a

I had always been attracted to the overly romanticized image of the penniless traveler. I wanted that life, or at least a taste of it. Being entirely independent sounded glorious; I wanted to go without knowing where I would end up, and I wanted to do it alone. I can't honestly say *why* I wanted that life—I'm a social person at heart. I guess I gravitated towards what I was not.

The image was persistent enough, though, that I made time to pursue it. I reserved the last week of a two-month study trip to Seville, Spain, for travel. The only planning I did was to create a cheat sheet of cheap hostels. Cordoba, my first stop, is a relatively small town compared to the others on my agenda, so my cheat sheet held only three hostels. The trip was short—about a thirty-minute train ride from Seville—and I started calling the hostels as soon as I got there. The first: *completo*. The second: just as full as the first. The third: no answer. And then the panic started.

I did find a place eventually, but the seeds of doubt had already taken root. No longer was I convinced that the "penniless traveler" lifestyle was for me.

Next on my trip was a visit to Madrid. Madrid is about forty times bigger than Cordoba, so I had ten hostels on my cheat sheet. I decided to call ahead, find a place to stay, calm my nerves. But, miraculously, every last hostel was full. *Completo*. I hated that word.

I arrived at the train station hours earlier than I needed to. I had a one-track mind: would I end up on the streets that night? I took out my journal and tried to write, but it was in vain. I got through one page then slammed it shut, writing, "¡Ayúdame, Dios!" Help me, God! Nothing I did stopped the fear. Worse, I was starting to get angry with God. How could He leave me here to rot?

Finally, the platform doors swung open. I dropped a few coins into a vending machine, hoping for solace in the ice cream bar. Solace, I found, but not in the ice cream. As I took the first bite, a man with a thick accent, a mix between British and Indian, greeted me in English.

"Are you traveling to Madrid?" he asked.

I told him I was; he was, too, just for one night. He asked if I had a place to stay; he didn't either. So, he suggested, why didn't we team up? Find a place to stay together? After all, double rooms are cheaper than singles.

Fear had blindfolded me, but God saw exactly what I needed: an angel, a Pakistani tourist, a friend. We found a place to stay that night, a cheap place in an ideal location. God wanted to show me that even in the situations that seem most desolate to us, He's just a glance away. No method is too big for God; no method is too small. He works for us in ways we never expect.

Four days later, I was on a plane to Paris. I slept like a baby the whole way.

DAY 33

LIVONIA, AGE 28

God will wipe every tear from their eyes. There will be no more death or mourning or crying or pain, for the old order of things has passed away.

Revelation 21:4

I met Bryan in elementary school. Our last names were so similar—mine was Fint; his was Fink—that we did everything together: sat together, stood in line together, and got in trouble for talking together.

The summer before we were to go to high school, Bryan was diagnosed with inoperable brain tumors. "God, why Bryan? Take me! Bryan has so much left to do. He's only fifteen. I'll die, if someone has to. I'll suffer. Lord, take me." There was only silence. "God, where are you? Why won't you answer me? I know you hear me."

While Bryan was in the hospital taking chemotherapy, I was studying. Bryan never attended classes, so I went to visit him on the weekends he was home. I remember watching him as he sat down on the porch swing with his water pistol aimed and ready to drench the first person that happened to walk out the screen door. He crookedly smiled when his sister entered the path of his water pistol. "I'll get you now!" he exclaimed as he jumped up and squirted her before she ran around the house out of his reach. He was too weak to chase her, but that didn't bother him. He grinned and went into the kitchen and ate the chocolate off the cookies his mom had made.

"I prayed day and night, God, for you to spare him. Why didn't you answer my prayers?" It was raining the day of Bryan's funeral and it was like even God Himself was crying. As I approached the casket for the last viewing, tears poured down my face. He seemed so peaceful. Even now, he had a smile on his face. Bryan's sister sang a song by Michael W. Smith. "I hear Bryan, singing in Heaven tonight, and in between the sadness, I hear Bryan, telling me that he's all right." Those precious words filled my soul. At that moment, I realized that God had answered my prayers—just not the way I had expected.

God's will is that there be no more sickness, death, mourning, crying, or pain. I prayed for God's will to be done on Earth, but God's will was fulfilled for Bryan by taking him to Heaven. I do not know why Bryan lived such a short life here on Earth, but I'm sure he would not trade one minute in Heaven for any amount of time on Earth. Bryan was a very brave person. He taught me that God's will is not always our will, but we must learn to go on and take the best parts of our loved ones with us.

For me, I'll never forget Bryan's smile.

In Loving Memory of Bryan Vincent Fink
Born: February 26, 1975
Died: April 6, 1991

95

DAY 34

KIMBERLEY, AGE 13, AUSTRALIA

Do not conform any longer to the pattern of this world, but be transformed by the renewing of your mind. Then you will be able to test and approve what God's will is—his good, pleasing and perfect will.

Romans 12:2

It all began as Camp Explosion finally arrived. The camp was fun, powerful, and phenomenal, as our guest speaker, Michael Guglielmucci, shared with us the things he went through in his past and the things he did for God. As he shared how he witnessed and saw his entire high school saved, it made me realize how powerful God really is.

I thought, "Why keep it to myself? Why have the best thing in the world and keep it as a secret?" Since this encounter, I finally got the drift that Jesus didn't just die for me; He died for the lost and those who don't know Him.

God took me through some serious self-readjusting. He put all the people I know who aren't saved on my heart.

And then he gave me an idea: to proclaim Christ's salvation at my school chapel and challenge the high school to choose their destiny.

When the big day arrived, I walked up to the stage with my palms sweaty and shaking. I stood behind the podium and surveyed the hundreds of faces in the audience, all staring back at me, wondering what I would say.

"My words really can't express the way I feel about Jesus' love and the compassion He has for every one of you in this place," I told them. "He is just crying out to you, and He wants you to stop and come to Him. God is here and He is the only one who cares for you 100 percent. He is the only one who will always be there when your heart is broken and you feel like giving up."

I shared with my classmates that accepting Christ is a decision we make for ourselves.

"Think about it," I challenged them. "If you were walking home and a car suddenly hit you, where do you think you personally would go? Heaven or Hell?"

What the world has to offer us is nothing in comparison to what we will experience in eternal life. It's not up to your friends or anyone else. You choose where you will go.

I continued on to identify and expose many areas where people are hurting. I spoke about loneliness, rejection, failure, and broken relationships. I spoke God's words of hope from Jeremiah as He assures us that He has a future and a hope for all those who follow Him.

After my talk in chapel was over, I was amazed that I actually heard God's will for me and that I obeyed him by putting His commands into action. I am only thirteen and a half, but I know I'm not going be shaken as I put my trust in Him. Since I spoke in chapel, I use every possible opportunity to share how awesome God is. My Jesus is closer than any other friend, and He has never once let me down.

DAY 35

MELISSA, AGE 20

Therefore confess your sins to each other, and pray for each other, so that you may be healed. The prayer of a righteous man is powerful and effective.

James 5:16

Her name is Denise, but I like to call her Faith. I met her my first year at the University of Virginia, a friend of a friend. She helped me with my photography project, and later we'd meet for lunch and I'd answer her questions about God. "What about other religions?" "Can you remind me why Jesus is the only way?" "How do you know?" Sometimes it was frustrating trying to explain and I felt like giving up. We're both Americans, but the words I spoke were another language to her. The Bible read like fiction. I began to pray for her. Amazingly, she prayed too, even when I'd not think of it. "You don't have a ride home? Let's pray about it," she'd say, and then close her eyes in the middle of a crowd, praying loud enough for them to wonder what in the world we were doing. I was baffled by her boldness. Her prayers were answered, and she didn't even believe Christ was God.

One evening Denise had so many doubts I felt it was impossible to connect. I prayed. I began to share stories from my life—how God had been there all along, even when I was lost. Denise began to open up also. She asked why Jesus was the Sacrificial Lamb. I showed her some Scriptures, but it wasn't until she took a step of faith and called Jesus "Lord" that God opened the eyes of her heart. "Oh! Now I see…" she said. "Without blood there is no forgiveness of sins. I understand."

I smiled. "From now on, I'm going to call you Faith." That night Faith gave her life to Christ.

This summer we live together, her room a door from mine. I greet her before class each morning, and at night we'll pray together. But she's noticed something different about me. "You don't ask how I'm doing," she says. "Faith," I begin, impatiently forming some excuse about time. She's waiting for me to tell me her what's wrong. But I can't. I am supposed to be her leader. How can I tell her I am being too proud to pray or read or listen to God?

Tonight we lay on the carpet, Bibles open. I am quiet, mostly, flipping through familiar pages, reading a little. Faith is praying silently. I can always tell. I turn to 1 Corinthians 13, to Ephesians, then 1 Timothy, John, James, randomly. The more I read, the more I am convicted. I have not been real with her; I'm feigning righteousness. I begin to weep and she waits. I pour myself out to her. This is not easy.

She receives me with Christlike forgiveness. "God answered my prayer for you," she says. We pray again, for our families and friends. This time my heart is humbled, believing, united with hers. If God can reconcile not only us to Him, but ourselves with each other, whispers my heart, truly He can do all things.

DAY 36

KEVIN, AGE 22

"Be still, and know that I am God."

Psalm 46:10

Arriving in a foreign country to study for the summer is about as relaxing as being dropped by military helicopter into the middle of a machine-gun battle. I discovered this firsthand during my time in Germany. I was suddenly immersed in a foreign culture, communicating almost exclusively in a foreign language, and trying to find my way around a new city. It all made me worrisome, impatient, and disoriented. I had to sleep more than usual so my mind could process the new environment and internalize lessons like not walking on the red part of the sidewalk because it was reserved for bicycles only. Even after much of the trip had passed I was still tired and confused by the rhythm of daily life in this foreign place.

One day, as I continued to wallow in my culture shock, I walked into a church—the city cathedral. After the door shut behind me, the bustling city outside hushed and all was silent. A lone red candle glowed softly in the front of the sanctuary to indicate that I was in the presence of Jesus. My eyes darted about the ornaments of the cathedral and came to rest on a large statue of Mary holding Jesus after His crucifixion. Jesus lay limp and covered in bloody wounds after his agony-filled Passion. I stepped closer and looked at Mary's face. Rather than looking angry or revengeful for the brutal death of her son, there was a serenity in her eyes. I reached out to touch the red wounds of Christ's feet. As my hand rested on the cold stone, I felt a fraction of the sorrow Mary must've felt when she held her murdered son. Yet along with the sorrow, I felt the sense of peace I saw on Mary's face—peace that comes from trust in the sovereign plan of Almighty God.

I thought how irritated and impatient I had been with this new culture. I thought how I allowed little things like not being able to understand everything my host family said at dinner to fill my day with worry. I knew Mary's grief was millions of times more difficult than my situation, yet she was so peaceful. She had nothing more than complete trust in the divine will of Almighty God. I knew that I wanted to trust more in the sovereignty of God, so in the silence I knelt to pray and the Lord filled me with His peace as I left the cathedral.

That statue has become for me a powerful image of trust in God's sovereignty. Even if I do not know my way around this foreign city, or the path of my own life, God does. I let Him direct, rather than force myself to understand everything going on around me. I have found that there is great peace in being still and knowing that God is God.

DAY 37

MARTHA, AGE 22

Therefore go and make disciples of all nations, baptizing them in the name of the Father and of the Son, and of the Holy Spirit, and teaching them to obey everything I have commanded you.

Matthew 28:19-20

Most of my family members are intellectual atheists. They will passionately tell you why they don't believe in God. When I became a Christian in high school, I thought I could keep my family life and my life with Jesus separate. I'd think, "I don't want to tell my intimidating, atheistic family that I believe in Jesus. What if telling them makes enjoyable, comfortable relationships change for the worst?" I was scared.

My Aunt Vicki did not have kids of her own so she and I became very close over the years. I loved spending time with her, laughing, talking about books, etc. However, I never told her about my relationship with God and the great joy He brings me. I worried that if I had, she'd think less of me, and our wonderful relationship would change.

I'll never forget one night when my mom, sister, and I were sitting on the couch at home talking and laughing. The phone rang and Mom picked it up.

"Hello?"

She was silent for a moment, and then her face dropped.

"The hospital? Right now?"

She hung up the phone.

"Vicki is dying."

She explained that Vicki had suffered a brain aneurysm and probably wouldn't be alive much longer. I saw Vicki's body at the hospital a few minutes later, but she clearly was no longer there. I held her small hands. I thought of how in a few hours the machines would be off. Vicki would be dead. Then my mind turned to her atheism. Could I find comfort in the image of Vicki spending eternity with God? No. All I could think about was how she would most likely spend eternity separated from her Creator. It was almost more than I could bear. I'd never once told Vicki about God, but I'd told her of countless new movies and restaurants that she should check out. I always thought I'd have time to grow more comfortable sharing my faith. When it came to telling Vicki about God, time had run out.

It's been three years since Vicki died. I still miss her and love her very much. I also still think of how I missed out on at least offering her the greatest gift possible. I loved her so I should have told her about my relationship with God through Christ. However, Vicki's death did teach me the importance of sharing my faith with the people I love *now*.

There may not be a later. Telling people about God and giving them the opportunity to respond to Him is the greatest privilege we have in this life. I hope to never let it pass me by again.

Since Vicki's death I have frequently shared my faith with my family. There have been no conversions, but I know that they have heard the Gospel and are aware of God's work in my life. I can only continue to obey Him by sharing with and praying for my family.

DAY 38

SARAH, AGE 18

Trust in the Lord with all your heart, and lean not on your own understanding. In all your ways acknowledge Him and He shall direct your path.

Proverbs 3:5-6

The rush came around seven, and I started with the most difficult table in the world. A sweet man could not have been more excited to buy dinner for his son and two friends. He took twenty minutes to write down everything their little hearts desired, which consisted of absolutely nothing that was actually on the menu. He read the list slowly, taking time between each item to wink at the appropriate little boy. By the time he finished, I had four tables waiting, and twenty more minutes passed while I tried to figure out how on Earth to put his order into the computer so the cooks would have some idea of what to make. Finally, I returned to my other frustrated tables only to discover they were all equally incapable of deciding what to eat in a reasonable time period. I stood at table number two for at least fifteen minutes listening to a mother and daughter argue over which salad dressing to get, then moved to table number three where an older couple refused to order until something was done about the flies. They continued to violently whack at them with their menus while I cleared a new table. Eventually, I slipped over to table number four, a group of soft-spoken Chinese-Americans; they spoke almost no English.

When I finally returned to the kitchen, I passed between two other waitresses named Laura and Beth. Beth was leaning leisurely against the countertop sharing her testimony. Beth had simultaneously become a blessing as well as a huge struggle for me. She was only two weeks into her career at the International House of Pancakes and she was already finding time to share her testimony, while I was running around with a dirty dishrag and a pocket full of dead flies. I swallowed my frustration and grabbed a plate of hot eggs. I was honestly excited that Beth would have the opportunity to share her faith, and equally resolved to the fact that I was being of very little help to God in this service. I could keep a smile on my face, but that was about it.

After another hour or so of running back and forth between tables, and retrieving everything from "toastier English muffins" to half of a to-go box, my first and most difficult table finally left. With a sigh of relief I began to clear the table, and found a whole lot more then dirty dishes. Scrawled in red crayon, the man had left a note on a napkin:

Ms. Sarah, Thank you very much for your kindness to us.

"You will know them by their love."—Jesus

"Love is a verb."—DC Talk.

My smile was a bit brighter the rest of the night; every-thing that had bothered me so much earlier seemed to have been left under the old man's menu with all the dead flies. I didn't need to be concerned with how much God was using me compared to Beth, and I shouldn't have assumed that just because her service to the Lord seemed more obvious to me that God had no place for me at IHOP. God has a different purpose for us all. It's not always easy for us to see, but our doubting moments are when we need to trust Him the most.

DAY 39

My sheep listen to my voice; I know them, and they follow me. I will give them eternal life, and they shall never perish. No one can snatch them out of my hand.

John 10:27-28

I needed a vacation. My friend Robert and I decided to take advantage of an upcoming three-day weekend to plan a drive up to Toronto. It was on. I booked the hotel room, got directions, and checked Toronto's website for the hot-spots to hang out. As the departure date grew near, we became more and more excited.

Then Matt called. Matt was a close friend of both Robert and me, and had moved to St. Louis three years earlier to go to medical school. Matt had always been the "strong Christian" in our group of friends, but since he had moved away, he had begun dealing with loneliness through drinking and sexual sin. Matt called that night to tell me that his girlfriend was pregnant, and that she was moving in with him. I was floored. Right there on the phone I started crying for my friend.

I felt in my heart that he should not marry this girl, at least not like this. She wasn't a Christian, and God commands us not to be unequally yoked. So I did one of the craziest things I've ever done. Following what I felt God wanted us to do, Robert and I cancelled our reservations in Toronto and drove south instead of north.

After spending the weekend hanging out with Matt, we took him out to breakfast.

"I love you," I said, looking Matt in the eye. "And it's because I love you that we drove to St. Louis to plead with you not to do what you are doing."

He put his fork down and looked up at me.

"I don't know exactly what the right answer is," I continued. "And I have no idea how you must be feeling, but I know that God will be faithful if you'll submit to Him."

There was a long, long pause.

"Well," he finally said. "Thanks for coming down. I know what you're saying is true, and I'll think about it, but I have to do what I have to do."

We laid hands on him, prayed for him, and drove home.

About a week later, Matt called me and told me that he was not going to live with his girlfriend—at least not yet. It was a hard decision because he felt responsible for her pregnancy, but he believed this was the path God was calling him to.

Last week I got another call from Matt. He said that he had been suspicious of his girlfriend's faithfulness while they were together, and decided to have the baby's DNA tested. He had just got the test results back, and the baby was not his. Again, I was floored. I thought back to the day that God spoke to me and told me to drive to St. Louis and tell him not to marry her. I was so thankful that Jesus had spoken to me, and in awe of how He watches over His flock when they are willing to submit to Him.

DAY 40

CHRIS, AGE 19

For since death came through a man, the resurrection of the dead comes also through a man. For as in Adam all die, so in Christ all will be made alive.

1 Corinthians 15:21-22

"Hi, Chris." Mom and Dad smiled at me from their position within the family garden.

I approached the perimeter of the garden with a confident inquisitiveness that only a strong-willed, three-year-old boy can have. I paused outside one of the rows, carefully watching my parents work among the tangle of sprouting vegetable plants.

"Now, Chris, you know the rule," my dad said, holding a large white bucket. "You can watch from out in the lawn, but I don't want you to walk in the garden."

"Why?"

Like many young children, it was my favorite question.

"Because you might accidentally step on one of the plants."

I stared into the garden, imagining myself walking through the rows.

"And one more thing." Dad reached into the bucket, pulled out a scoop full of a white powdery substance, and resumed sprinkling it on the plants. "You see this white powder stuff?"

I nodded, mesmerized as I watched it float through the air in cloudlike puffs.

"Do not..." He paused, making sure he had my attention. "*Do not* put this stuff in your mouth, okay?"

"Why?" I asked again.

"Because it's poison—it's supposed to keep the bugs from eating the plants. It could really harm you, so don't touch it or get it in your mouth, or anything like that, understand?"

I responded by firmly stepping into the garden, dipping my finger into a freshly sprinkled mound of the white powder, and licking it off of my finger.

My parents stared in horror, utterly dumbfounded by my direct and blatant insubordination.

I began to cry.

It has been said that foolishness is bound up in the heart of a child, and I don't disagree. I cannot help but laugh every time I remember that early act of blatant—and almost fatal—disobedience. I don't recall much of the events that followed: all I remember is crying in my father's arms, as he and my mother gave me the vomit inducing medicine that removed the poison from my digestive system. On one level, it's hard for me to imagine being so rebellious at such an early age. On another level, however, I'm not surprised at all. Like the poison I ingested, sin is deadly, and it strikes early. Every time I reminisce about the "garden incident," I am reminded of the sin in my own life, and of my perpetual need for a Savior.

Sin is real, yes—but salvation is an even greater reality. Because of Adam and Eve's disobedience in the Garden of Eden, sin entered the world. Because of Christ's obedience on the cross, however, eternal life was restored. Through one man came sin and death. Through an infinitely greater Man came forgiveness and life-giving love.

It is in this faith, and with this hope, that I live each day.

How to Follow Jesus

Brad Huddleston

I was a thief.

There's no nicer way to say it or I would. When I was about eleven, I would go into stores and steal things. Sometimes I would act alone. Sometimes I would act with friends.

But all of that changed on an Easter Sunday morning. I was sitting in church as usual; however, that day was anything but usual. I felt a sense that I was being irresistibly pulled toward something. Even now it's hard to fully describe the feeling. The pull was so strong that I didn't hear a word of my pastor's sermon. At the end of his message, he invited those who wanted to accept Jesus as their Savior to come to the front of the church. The "pull" drew me to the front where my Uncle Skip greeted me and helped me to ask Jesus to come into my heart and forgive my sins. I had always heard people tell stories of their "salvation" experience and how wonderful they felt.

Well, my story is different. I felt worse.

When I returned home and walked into my bedroom, it seemed as though some of the objects around me were glowing as if they were shrouded in a yellow haze. I quickly realized that the "glowing" objects were things I had stolen. Immediately, I had an unmistakable urge to take all of those objects back to the stores and pay for them.

There was a problem, however. In fact, there were several problems. For one thing, I didn't want to. Furthermore, I had no money and I had eaten most of what I had stolen. The urge wouldn't leave, though, so I sought out my grandfather for advice. I was painfully embarrassed to go to him.

Perhaps you've learned that the Bible teaches that Jesus is at the right hand of the Father. Well, I used to think that my grandfather was at the right hand of Jesus! So I felt sick at the thought of him learning such terrible news about me. In the end, I went to him because I simply couldn't take it anymore; I had to tell someone.

"Granddad," I said, "I know you'll be ashamed of me and I really don't want to tell you this but I have to. I've stolen some things and I think I'm supposed to take them back to the stores, ask for forgiveness, and pay for what I've taken."

What do you suppose a wise grandfather would say? "Forget about it, son. God has already forgiven you," or "It's no big deal; you're just a kid, so forget about it." My granddad's words were different. And they changed my life forever. He said, "Son, God is talking to you and you should listen." (I cringed. *You've got to be kidding,* I thought.) "But I have no money," I explained. "Plus, I've eaten most of it. This is embarrassing."

"I'll tell you what," Granddad said. "Get several bags, one to represent each store. Gather up what you have left and I'll go with you. We'll go to each store, you ask for the manager, tell him what you've done wrong, offer to pay for it, and I'll take care of the bill."

So off we went. I remember handing the manager of K-Mart the bag of stolen goods and telling him that I'd just asked Jesus to come into my heart. I asked his forgiveness and said that if he wanted any money, my granddad would pay the bill. None of the five store managers that I spoke to wanted any money. In fact, most of them looked like they wanted to hug me. After Granddad and I left the last store, I felt clean. I felt free. I felt like those other people I had heard talking about the joy of their salvation experience.

Granddad was the first person to actually demonstrate to me what Jesus is really like. My granddad took my shame on him. After all, he wasn't the one who stole, yet there he stood with his hand on my shoulder, in public, bearing my humiliation. Jesus did the same thing for the entire human race. He willingly allowed Himself to be humiliated for sins He didn't commit. My granddad also gave me a first-person look at what it meant for Jesus to pay a bill He didn't owe. Granddaddy Charlie was willing to pay for something he didn't owe. Although my granddad didn't have to pay anything that day, I learned that Jesus did pay the ultimate price and, as a result, I was forgiven. I will never ever have to pay for those sins. That's what Jesus is all about. My life was forever changed because I saw that in Granddad that humiliating day.

God is our Father, and thankfully, He has a different view of things. God so loved the human race that He allowed His only Son to die for you. Like it or not, God makes the rules. You can find out about God and what He has to say to you by reading a book He wrote called the Bible. When you read the Bible, you are actually finding out what God wants to communicate to you. It's the only book ever written that is perfect. God wrote the Bible, not just to the entire human race, but also to me and to you as individuals.

In the Bible, we learn about *sin*. Sin means to *miss the mark*. It's like shooting at a target and not hitting the bull's eye. The bull's eye represents all of God's expectations of us. When we don't make a perfect score, we sin. The result is guilt. All people sense this guilt, even those who don't read the Bible or know God. The reason we all have that feeling is because we are guilty! Each of us fails to measure up to God's standards. Simply put, we all sin (do wrong things) and fall short of God's expectations and are therefore guilty.

You are not capable of hitting the mark without God's help. That's where Jesus came in; and it's why you can't be free from sin and guilt without Him. Prior to Jesus' death two thousand years ago, people obtained forgiveness of sins by giving up their most valuable possession. Their valuable treasure most often was a lamb. In order to have their sins forgiven, they had to shed the blood of their most perfect lamb or die themselves. Jesus is God's Son. God decided He would take care of the sin problem Himself by sending His Son into the world as a "Lamb" who would die on a cross and pay the full price for sin, taking away the sins, once and for all, of everyone who will put his or her trust in Jesus.

The ultimate penalty for *not* accepting God's provision of forgiveness, through His Son Jesus, is death. The Bible says…

For the wages of sin is death. (Romans 6:23)

119

Death means that those whose sins are not forgiven will spend all eternity in a place called Hell, a place Jesus talked a lot about while He was on Earth. Hell is not a party. According to God's Book, people who go there will be separated from God and everyone else. It will be like solitary confinement in a furnace forever and ever. Hell is where loneliness and pain get free reign, without the limits of time or forgiveness.

This is the bad news. Now let me tell you the Good News. You can have forgiveness of your sins. It is a free gift to all who ask.

> *For it is by grace you have been saved, through faith—and this not from yourselves, it is the gift of God—not by works, so that no one can boast.* (Ephesians 2:8-9)

If you've not stopped reading by now, Jesus is knocking at your heart's door. He wants to be invited in so He can form a relationship with you.

> *Here I am! I stand at the door and knock. If anyone hears my voice and opens the door, I will come in and eat with him, and he with me.* (Revelation 3:20)

Although you don't physically see Jesus, He is there. He's like the wind: you don't see Him, but you know He's there. Why don't you invite Him to come into your heart right now?

> *Yet to all who received him, to those who believed in his name, he gave the right to become children of God.* (John 1:12)

If you would like to receive Jesus into your heart, you must stop sinning. It doesn't mean you become perfect the moment you ask Him to help you. Over time, Jesus will reveal your sins to you. He will then instruct you on how to overcome the sin and the temptation to go back to the way you used to live. And God has set up a way for you to maintain your relationship with Him and your freedom in Him forever—through Bible study and prayer. According to God's Word, you must also regularly meet with other Christians where the Bible is taught and where people worship God with great passion. God wants you to be in a church where you consistently feel the presence of the Holy Spirit. He has a powerful plan for your life. If you'd like to follow Jesus for the rest of your life, simply pray the following prayer…

> Dear Jesus, I ask that you enter into my heart and life and forgive me for sinning. Please reveal to me what my sins are and give me the power, strength, and freedom to stop sinning. I believe that you died for my sins and rose again on the third day. I commit my entire life to you. Please fill me with your Holy Spirit. I confess that Jesus is now my Lord. Amen.

If you prayed that prayer and meant it, please e-mail me at brad@bradradio.com. I'd like to encourage you.

Editor Bios

Brad Huddleston

Brad Huddleston is an Evangelist and lives in Singers Glen, Virginia with his wife, Beth. He has had the privilege of traveling to various parts of the United States, including his home region of Virginia. He has also conducted extensive revivals overseas, including Australia and New Zealand. This work has included retreats, churches, camps, community rallies, colleges, universities, Bible colleges, and public and private schools, and has spanned across various denominations. He frequently holds The Revival Generation Outpouring rallies in which groups from all denominations gather for intense worship, praise, and preaching.

Brad's call to ministry includes radio broadcasting. In 1990, he helped to plant our local contemporary Christian radio station, where he was program director and morning show host. This became a platform for Brad to begin his preaching/revival ministry. Although he no longer works in full-time radio, he still hosts Revival Generation Worship—a two-hour weekly praise and worship show. Because of digital technology and the Internet, Brad is able to produce and host this show from anywhere in the world. He also owns a multimedia production company, Brad Huddleston Productions.

If you are interested in having Brad speak to your group, contact him at brad@bradradio.com His website is www.bradradio.com.

Brian Hamilton

Brian Hamilton works behind the scenes most of the time, finding fun and refuge in his Web development work. He co-founded, designed, and developed Pew-Fellows.com, a public forum for Christian youth to discuss their questions, aside from maintaining his own personal website. He continues to work as a freelance XHTML and PHP developer for a wide variety of sites.

Brian's other passions include music and language. Languages are doubtlessly his academic forte; his high school studies culminated with a two-month study trip to Seville, Spain. He is conversationally fluent in Spanish, and can handle advanced French. Now, at eighteen years old, Brian looks forward to beginning college life at Messiah College in the fall of 2003, where he plans to major in computer science.

His website is www.bdhamilton.com.

Josh Sundquist

After Joshua Sundquist lost his left leg to cancer at age nine, he began speaking in front of groups about his experiences. He has since touched the lives of thousands as he has spoken at schools, businesses, and even the National Press Club and the White House. At eighteen, he is one of the youngest people ever to be accepted as a member of the National Speaker's Association.

Josh has been the national spokesperson for the Combined Federal Campaign, and through his involvement, millions of dollars were raised for charities all over the world. Josh is an honorary member of Lance Armstrong's U.S. Postal Service Cycling Team, and a member of the Winter Park Disabled Ski Team.

He has won numerous national awards for his writing in magazines, his column in the *Richmond Times Dispatch*, and his pieces in *Daily Guideposts*. Currently, he is training to ski race in the Paralympics, and he attends the College of William and Mary during the off-season.

His website is www.JoshSundquist.com.

Writer Profiles

(in alphabetical order by first name)

BEN LAMB, 18

Harrisonburg, Virginia

The mission of my life is to find God's mission for me. If God calls me to preach, I'll preach; if He calls me to serve soup, I'll get my soup-spoon; if He calls me to write, then I'll scribble some random thoughts and try to get them published in devotional books like this. I am a vegetarian, I play piano, and am an ultimate-frisbee fanatic. Currently, I live in Denver, Colorado, as a part of a year-long service program called Discipleship, Encounter, Outreach (DEO). My home congregation is Community Mennonite Church in Harrisonburg, Virginia. E-mail: blamb147@yahoo.com.

BETH, 23

Harrisonburg, Virginia

My life has been far from normal, but through the strangeness God has given me many stories to tell. He has truly changed my life, and He has made my life worth living.

Hidden Talent: I am fluent in three languages (four if you count pig Latin).

If you had three wishes, you would want: 1) Enough money to start a home for disadvantaged kids. 2) The ability to speak and understand every language. 3) Telekinesis.

On Friday nights, I usually: Stay up late playing cards with my friends.

In ten years, I see myself: Serving God wherever He puts me.

BRAD DeBLOIS, 19

Hometown? I don't understand.

Born, moved around (Dad was in military), high school in northern Virginia, now doing the college thing.

Hidden Talent: I try not to hide my talents.

Word or phrase most often overused: Excellent.

If you had three wishes, you would want: 1) Money—it opens possibilites in life. 2) I'd like to be able to fly. 3) Finally, I'd like a Q&A session with God.

On Friday nights, I usually: Go on a date—too bad it doesn't happen very often.

In ten years, I see myself: I like to think that I don't know exactly where I'll be ten years from now. Although I would like to be married with kids on the way.

BRIAN HAMILTON, 18

Harrisonburg, Virginia

Brian Hamilton works behind the scenes most of the time, finding fun and refuge in his Web development work. He co-founded, designed, and developed Pew-Fellows (http://pew-fellows.com), a public forum for Christian youth to discuss their questions, aside from maintaining his own personal website (http://bdhamilton.com). He continues to work as a freelance XHTML and PHP developer for a wide variety of sites. Brian's other passions include music and language. Languages are doubtlessly his academic forte; his high-school studies culminated with a two-month study trip to Seville, Spain. He is conversationally fluent in Spanish, and can handle advanced French. He aspires to play piano like Gershwin and the guitar like Brad

Yoder. Now, at eighteen years old, Brian looks forward to beginning college life at Messiah College in the fall of 2003 where he plans to major in computer science.

CASSIE ARNOLD, 13
Harrisonburg, Virginia
Hidden Talent: If I told you, then it wouldn't really be hidden. Would it?
Word or phrase most often overused: Dude!
On Friday nights, I usually: Spend time with either my family or my friends (watching a movie, playing board games, talking, etc.).
In ten years, I see myself: On the mission field.

CHRISTOPHER CUDDY, 19
Apollo, Pennsylvania
Chris was born at an orphanage in Seoul, South Korea, in 1984. He was adopted at three months of age, and was reared in a loving Christian home. He was home-schooled from first through tenth grade, and he attended public school during his junior year of high school. He went on to complete his high-school education at The Kiski School (www.kiski.org), "the oldest boy's boarding school in the United States." He graduated from Kiski in 2002, and has been included in several editions of *Who's Who among American High School Students*. Chris lives in the Pittsburgh area with his parents and four younger sisters. He is currently a sophomore at The Franciscan University of Steubenville, where he majoring in theology and philosophy. He is also a research assistant at the St. Paul Center for Biblical Theology (www.salvationhistory.com), and is a contributor to various journals and magazines that specialize in theology, apologetics, and evangelization. Chris loves to get mail, and can be reached at ChristopherJCuddy@hotmail.com.
Hidden Talent: Beat-boxing in the shower.
Word or phrase most often overused: "Good sweet!!!" (A phrase that communicates strong surprise, shock, and/or unrest.)

On Friday nights, I usually: Read, write, hang out with friends, listen to music, and watch movies.

In ten years, I see myself: Teaching, writing, and speaking.

DAN HAMMER, 21
Annapolis, Maryland

I was born and raised until the age of thirteen in Richmond, Virginia. My dad changed jobs, and my family moved to Annapolis, Maryland, when I was entering the eigth grade. I played basketball and lacrosse in high school. I am currently a senior at the College of William and Mary, and I'm majoring in economics and business. I work for the sports information department at W&M, and I just finished my summer internship at US Lacrosse in Baltimore, Maryland. I accepted Christ as my Savior at age eight, and have been trying my best to live for Him ever since. I am twenty-one years old currently.

Hidden Talent: I'm a great public address announcer.

Word or phrase most often overused: Awesome!

If you had three wishes, you would: 1) Become a college basketball coach. 2) Have season tickets to the Redskins. 3) Ask for there to be no traffic whenever I drive.

On Friday nights, I usually: Hang out with my friends doing whatever.

In ten years, I see myself: Trying to follow God's will for my life. Possibly married with kids. Hopefully working in sports somewhere.

DAVID TIECHE, 27
San Jose, California

David Tieche, who is twenty-seven, grew up in Ohio, went to college in Indiana, was a missionary for Youth For Christ in Hawaii, worked for the air force, and was a pioneering member of the San Jose Teacher Project, a program that recruits business professionals to teach in underperforming public schools in the Bay Area. David teaches high-school English at Gunderson High School. He is also helps lead the drama ministry at Family Community Church in San Jose, and is a frequent speaker at the church's mid-week services. He lives in downtown San Jose with his wife, Nicole, and their cat, Madison. He's not really a cat person, though.

Hidden Talent: I have the unique ability to enthusiastically misuse large words (penultimate, for example) but use them in ways that make other people understand what I'm saying. I also make a mean waffle.

If you had three wishes, you would want: For the AIDS virus to mutate instantly into something as innocuous as the common cold; for teacher's salaries to be bolstered so that the profession could attract good, passionate, and caring people; and for enough money to produce thoughtful, intelligent, and moral entertainment options for Americans, who for years have been subjected to Adam Sandler movies.

On Friday nights, I usually: Hang out with my wife.

FELIX J. LOCKHART, 18
Harrisonburg, Virginia

Well, I'm a self-taught computer technician, freelance writer, musician, and I used to be a counselor. Not bad for being only eighteen, eh?

Hidden Talent: Singing/composition.

Word or phrase most often overused: I try to vary my words as much as possible (thanks to English class), but I do tend to overuse parentheses.

If you had three wishes, you would want: Hmm, I'd probably ask for some money, and then tell the genie to give the other two wishes to someone else.

On Friday nights, I usually: Drive around randomly.

In ten years, I see myself: Working as a computer technician with 2.5 kids (also known as average).

GRAHAM ROUSE, 24

Columbus, Ohio

C'mon. I just spent an hour trying to shave one episode of my life down to 500 words for this book. You don't want me to get started on my life story.

Hidden Talent: I can roll my stomach (in both directions).

Word or phrase most often overused: Strizzle.

If you had three wishes, you would want: 1) Mad wisdom. 2) Mad integrity. 3) Mad money.

On Friday nights, I usually: Friday night is "date night" with my girlfriend (hopefully fiancée by the time this book is published), and it is always my favorite night of the week.

In ten years, I see myself: Teaching English (in Africa?).

JBJ, 15

Mackay, Queensland, Australia

I was born in Seoul, South Korea, in 1988 and then was adopted by a Christian, Aussie family who are awesome and totally amazing parents and are pastors of a rockin' church in Mackay (which is on the coast in tropical North Queensland.) I'm an only child, and I'm in year eleven at school. I love art, music, singing, my friends, my family, and my life...which has Jesus in it. I'm presently an assistant leader in a cell full of beautiful girls of God, and go to an absolutely awesome youth group. I love you guys!!!

Hidden Talent: I can play air-guitar REALLY well.

Word or phrase most often overused: "OH COOL!" and "AWESOME!"

If you had three wishes, you would ask: 1) That school would start at a reasonable hour of 12:00 in the afternoon (so I can sleep in). 2) That maths would never be boring and soooo unexciting. 3) That chocolate and junk food would never make you have zits or make you put on weight!

On Friday nights, I usually: Go to youth, man! And then afterwards, go and chill out at MacDonald's with all my mates!

In ten years, I see myself: I'd like to see myself in the media or design world, creating and designing things, and I hope to be speaking or working with young people and have a family of my own.

JIM STEVENS, 17
Harrisonburg, Virginia

Well, I'm a Harrisonburg native pretty much. Although I was born in Charleston, I moved here after only several years of life. I have been blessed to attend the same church for all of my time here in the 'Burg and have enjoyed it a lot. Life is good!

Word or phrase most often overused: Solid!

On Friday nights, I usually: Hang out with my friends playing poker or watching a movie.

JOHN BEEDE, 21
Las Vegas, Nevada

Growing up in Las Vegas, Nevada, John gave his first performance when he was four years old. It was to his little brother and the complete set of Ninja Turtle action figures. In high school, he directed and performed in a weekly comedy show and spoke to youth groups, schools, and churches all over the country. He has given dozens upon dozens of presentations to tens of thousands of people. The success lessons John can bring to your group are derived from his extraordinary experiences as an Eagle Scout, state champion in both debate and diving, class president, United States Senate page, camp counselor, and youth group leader. After receiving a BA in communications from Wheaton College, Illinois, John has been speaking to groups nationwide as the funniest youth speaker in America. The bottom line is: your audience will listen, relate, laugh, and grow as a result of John's performance. John Beede, P.O. Box 50366, Henderson, NV 89016; 702-809-2727; johnny@johnnybd.com.

Hidden Talent: I can make anyone laugh within one minute of meeting them.

Word or phrase most often overused: "Sweet action, tenaction."

If you had three wishes, you would want: 1) A solution to the AIDS epidemic. 2) All people on planet Earth to have a simultaneous, genuine belly laugh. 3) A 100% worldwide literacy rate.
On Friday nights, I usually: Perform stand-up comedy.
In ten years, I see myself: Hosting a late-night talk show.

JOSH SHIPP, 22 (DAY 30)

Los Gatos, California

Twenty-two-year-old Josh Shipp is a youth speaker for school assemblies, youth conferences, and Christian youth events. He is celebrating over five years of entertaining, inspiring, and empowering youth audiences nationwide. His message is simple, yet powerful. Entertaining, yet challenging. He has spoken to over half a million teens and has shared the stage with Bill Cosby. Abandoned, neglected, and abused as a child, Josh's personal story of triumph over tragedy through Christ inspires youth to overcome life's struggles and to live life to the fullest. Contact info: Josh Shipp Productions, P.O. Box 530, Los Gatos, CA 95031; www.joshshipp.com; 877-582-6898.

JOSH WHITE, 18 (DAY 13)

Troutville, Virginia

I was born in Salem, Virginia, where I was raised and grew into a fine young man. At age five I realized that Jesus Christ paid the price for my sins on the cross by bearing the nails in His hands and feet. I accepted Him as my personal Savior and Lord and it wasn't until I was about eleven that I truly started "living" for Him. I have been involved with my church youth group ever since I was old enough. I have been out of the country once to the small Caribbean island of Saint Lucia, which is an amazingly poor place. I played tennis on my high-school tennis team all four years and thoroughly enjoy the sport. I am an avid music fan and listen to just about all types of music, with funky rock, emo, and alternative probably being my favorites. I attempt to play the guitar and am still learning, although I lead worship occassionally for my youth group. I just finished being a camp counselor at Grace Bible Camp for seven and a half weeks. It was one of the most amazing and influential summers of my life. God truly is amazing and my whole life story I am striving to let Him mold and make into something beautiful.

Hidden Talent: I can make sounds very similar to those of Chewbacca from *Star Wars*. I can attract women from all over the globe by turning on my "chick magnet" switch. Yeah, right, I think not.

If you had three wishes, you would: I would ask for the ability to fly just like Superman. I would just kick my heels and yell, "Up, up, and away," and away I'd go. I'd then proceed to fly to the small island that I would wish for second, and build a castle on the island. It would be somewhere I could "get away from it all." I would drink lemonade under the palm trees and listen to the waves in my newly sewed "Super Josh" suit, which my tailors at the castle had made for me. For my third and final wish, I would wish for enough money for the Grace Bible Camp chapel to be built and in full operation.

On Friday nights, I usually: Hang out with friends and just chill out after a long week. I enjoy talking to old friends, playing guitar with various people, listening to new tunes, cruising around being stupid, and playing Halo with a bunch of people. The more the merrier. I also enjoy riding four-wheelers at night and swimming during the summer months.

In ten years, I see myself: In ten years I will be twenty-eight years of age and probably married to a beautiful, godly woman. Hopefully I will have a job where I get to deal heavily with helping people and maybe traveling. I will have a dog and a Volkswagon camper bus that I can go to Alaska in. I've always had a dream and desire to go and explore Alaska. It seems like such an amazing state. By that time I might have a young Josh running around, but who knows, that is for God to know and me to find out!

JOSHUA SUNDQUIST, 19 (DAY 11)

Harrisonburg, Virginia (same as almost all the other authors in this book)

I once dyed my hair with Kool-Aid. Unfortunately you could smell it a lot better than you could see it, and my hair was very sticky until my next shower.

Hidden Talent: Freestyle rapping and disguising my voice for prank phone calls.

Word or phrase most often overused: "Hardcore," as in "Dude, that shower was hardcore," or "This has been a truly hardcore nap."

If you had three wishes, you would: 1) Eliminate the need for sleep. 2) Eliminate the need for eating. 3) Eliminate the need for small talk so that all conversasions could immediatly proceed to the meaning of life and why girls are so hard to understand/beautiful.

On Friday nights, I usually: Pull a practical joke and then join my assailants for a late-night discussion on the meaning of life and why girls are so hard to understand/beautiful.

In ten years, I see myself: Playing on the U.S. Amputee Soccer Team and giving motivational speeches.

P.S. My website is www.JoshSundquist.com. I am the first to admit that it needs to be updated, but it's my website nonetheless.

KATHRYN HAMILTON, 16

On Friday nights, I usually: I love to hang out with my friends doing any number of things, like walking, going to the mall, going to movies, and just sitting around listening to music.

In ten years, I see myself: I hope to be a chef at my own five-star resturant somewhere in South Carolina.

"KESLEY" JEFF M. SKELTON JR., 27

Pheonix, Arizona

Growing up, I lived in Illinios, Ohio, New Mexico, Arizona, and Virginia. Dad was in the navy until 2002, and Mom is a recovering alcoholic. I started drinking and using drugs at age ten, and by age thirteen my life took a real downhill turn. I was arrested for the first time, as well as jumped into a gang. As I graduated to harder drugs, I seemed to get into more trouble. At sixteen I was so strung out and unhappy with my life, I was admitted to my first treatment center for drug use and a suicide attempt. I stayed clean for a bit, but found myself in front of another judge by eighteen. After three rehabs, I was going to jail. I was given a five-year sentence, with half of it suspended. Only by the grace of God did I not have to serve all the time that was given to me. I was godless but clean for the next six and a half years. With a wife and a daughter, I found my addiction once again. Cocaine and heroin were the gods I bowed to. When I hit bottom I asked God to help me. With His help, another rehab, and my support system (my family and my church), God has carried me for almost two years, drug- and alcohol-free. I know it's not the longest I've been clean and sober, but it's the happiest I've ever been. I am currently a Bible-school student, and I know that God has something planned for my life, but I have to let Him be in control.

Hidden Talent: I am a master on things with wheels. I can't chew gum and stand at the same time for very long, but give me some wheels, and a ramp and I'm flyin'. I'm also a pretty good drummer.

Word or phrase most often overused: The phrase I prabably say way too much is WWWWWAASSSSSS UUUUUPPPP!

If you had three wishes, you would want: 1) No bills. 2) Not having to work. 3) Not to get tired and have to sleep.

On Friday nights, I usually: I spend Friday nights usually taking my wife and two daughters out to eat.

In ten years, I see myself: In ten years I want to be a strong, faithful man of God, in a place where God wants me to be.

Kevin Mayer, 22
Fairfax, Virginia
In ten years, I see myself: A husband and father.

Kristina Lewis, 17
Grottoes, Virginia
I was born in New York (not the city), grew up in Keezletown, Virginia, and now live in Grottoes. I am a crazy high-school senior who loves to read and play with little kids. I have spent the past year and a half giving God complete control over my life, and it has been truly AWESOME to see how much better of a job of it He does than I ever could!!
Hidden Talent: The ability to stay sane while teaching VBS with a classroom full of energetic pre-schoolers…and to enjoy it.
Word or phrase most often overused: What?!?!?
If you had three wishes, you would want: More time to sleep, more time to write, and more wishes!!
On Friday nights, I usually: Enjoy the fact that I don't have to do homework, hang out with family and friends, and write fun and encouraging letters to people.
In ten years, I see myself: Enjoying life, doing whatever God tells me to do, wherever He tells me to do it!!

Laura Leischner, 17
Harrisonburg, Virginia
Growing up in the sunny hill country of Luray, Virginia, I learned the importance of sunscreen at an early age. Since then I have consistently stayed pale and burn free. To keep my skin shaded from the sun, I avidly watch the television show *Price Is Right* with my dad and also play the card game gin with my mom. I occasionally go outside with SPF-50 suncreen and attend my church youth group, which I enjoy.
Hidden Talent: I have the knack for having the winning bid on vintage apparel from eBay.
Word or phrase most often overused: That's cr-azy.

If you had three wishes, you would want: A lifetime supply of Tropicana orange juice, an eternally clean bedroom, and the chance to meet Dave Matthews.

On Friday nights, I usually: I like to eat a lot of food, either with people or by myself; I do not have a preference.

In ten years, I see myself: I see myself as a youth pastor guiding teenagers towards a lifetime relationship with Christ and having a great time doing so.

LIVONIA FINT, 28
Fort Defiance, Virginia

I grew up in a Christian home and accepted Jesus into my heart and life when I was seven. My family is very close and we spend a lot of time together. I have one brother and one sister. I am the youngest. My sister, DeLeta, is married with three children: Jason, Cody, and Rachael. I live with my brother, West, who is leasing a dairy farm in Fort Defiance. My dad does most of the milking at West-Hope Dairy while my mom keeps us all in line. Before moving to Virginia, I lived in the small rural town of Aurora, West Virginia, for twenty-five years. Aurora is along Route 50 on top of Cheat Mountain near the Garrett County, Maryland border. I attended Bridgewater College for two and a half years before transferring to Garrett Community College, where I graduated with an associate's degree in office technology and a certificate in computer applications. In June 2000 I started working at AIMR, located in Charlottesville. Currently I am working as a quality assurance associate in the information systems department, testing Web- and Windows-based computer applications. My favorite color is purple and my favorite kind of music is Southern gospel. I teach Sunday school and work with junior- and senior-high youth at Middle River Church. I enjoy desktop publishing, learning how to use various computer applications, and, most importantly, writing. I have started writing several novels, and some day in the near future hope to have them published. I pray that all who read my devotional will find God's love and comfort in times of great sorrow.

On Friday nights, I usually: On a Friday nights I like to curl up on the couch and watch a good movie.

In ten years, I see myself: No matter how things may change over the years, one thing is sure: I will have a personal relationship with Jesus every day of my life. Within the next ten years, I want to be writing full-time. I have known even as a small child that God has called me to be a writer. It has been a long journey, but finally I feel like it is within my grasp. I am eagerly waiting for all that God has in store for my life. I know it will be better than anything I have imagined.

MARK STIES, 32

Richmond, Virginia (originally)

Mark Sties ("Stees") is a Christian recording artist. Mark's musical sojourn began in 1987 at the age of sixteen. Over the next several years he provided lead vocals and guitar for a number of bar bands in his hometown of Richmond, Virginia. In his early twenties, a life apart from God and disillusionment with the politics of the music industry led to clinical depression, obsessive-compulsive disorder, and an eating disorder, which nearly cost him his life. Overcoming that struggle, which he unashamedly attributes to his relationship with Jesus Christ, has resulted in prolific seasons of writing, recording, and live performance. As God directs, Mark continues to share his healing testimony in concert to youth and young adults in both Christian and secular venues. He has a BFA in fine craft from Virginia Commonwealth University and has received professional training in guitar, voice, and music theory at Christ for the Nations Institute in Dallas, Texas. Mark by vocation is a Web, graphic, and sound designer. He and his wife, Alison, currently make their home near South Bend, Indiana.

MARTHA BOONE ARMSTRONG, 22

Norfolk, Virginia

I grew up in Norfolk, Virginia, in a progressive, artsy neighborhood. I did the usual kids stuff—school, soccer teams, etc. Up until my parents' divorce my life was carefree. After the divorce a series of family problems ensued, but not everything was bad. On January 3, 1998, I became a Christian after months of getting to know some faithful believers and reading the Scriptures. God reconciled me to Himself through His Son by grace through faith. From 1999-2003, I attended the College of William and Mary, where I became very active in InterVarsity. God used IV and the amazing friends that I met to mature my faith during college. Now, I'm a recent graduate praying that God will teach me to trust Him to provide for me in the "real world."

Hidden Talent: Performing as my alter-ego, Supersaint. Supersaint is a "Christian" superhero (clad in a children's Superman suit) who possesses glaring faults intended to comically teach Christians to be honest, open, and willing to admit weakness. Supersaint also yells a lot, a special bonus in my mind.

Word or phrase most often overused: Spaz.

If you had three wishes, you would want: 1) To joyfully serve God to the best of my ability for the entirety of my life. 2) To stay in close touch with my friends from William and Mary. 3) For all people to have access to adequate food, health care, etc.

On Friday nights, I usually: Hang out with friends. What we do doesn't really matter, but if a Slurpee is involved I'm particularly happy.

In ten years, I see myself: Hopefully married with children and in a career that challenges me while making a difference in the world. I'm particularly interested in non-profit/social work.

MATTHEW SUNDQUIST, 16
Harrisonburg, Virginia

Word or phrase most often overused: Your mother.

On Friday nights, I usually: Keep it real; go driving.

In ten years, I see myself: In the Navy Seals, serving out my time after attending the naval academy.

P.S. My older brother, Josh, one of the editors of this book, is absolutely way awesome and totally cool, and may or may not have added this sentence himself during the editing process.

Micaela, 18

Harrisonburg, Virginia

I've lived in the Shenandoah Valley my entire life with both of my parents, my sister, and a plethora of pets. I enjoy traveling, reading, speaking French, and dancing.

Hidden Talent: I've danced for sixteen years, four of which I spent in a touring company—the Shenandoah Contemporary Dance Theatre. The SCDT has travelled to NYC to perform every year that I was involved.

On Friday nights, I usually: Somethin' crazy.

In ten years, I see myself: I hope to be a doctor.

Nicole Nutting, 16

Fraser, Colorado

I have two wonderful parents and three siblings, and I am proud to call the beautiful Rocky Mountains my home. I've been home-schooled almost all my life. I love anything to do with music: playing musical instruments, singing, composing, listening, etc.

Hidden Talent: I play soccer.

Word or phrase most often overused: Like.

On Friday nights, I usually: Hang out with family and/or friends, or read a good book.

In ten years, I see myself: Married and raising a family.

Rachel Pennington, 24

Oak Hill, West Virginia

I was adopted into a wonderful Christian family, raised in the Church, and went on to Asland University, where I majored in creative writing and religion. I accepted my first full-time ministry position at Mt. Olive Brethren Church, where I currently serve.

Hidden Talent: I can play acoustic guitar, piano, and drums.

Word or phrase most often overused: Snap yo!

If you had three wishes, you would want: My own personal amusement park, a house on the beach, and a lifetime supply of Starbucks coffee.

On Friday nights, I usually: Drink coffee at a local coffee shop, read, and relax.

In ten years, I see myself: God willing, speaking to large amounts of people, bringing them a word from the Lord in due season for their lives. I would also love to be writing and published.

REBEKAH BARKER, 20
Massanutten Village, VA

I was born in Winchester, Virginia. I received Christ when I was five years old. I live at home with my mom, who is my best friend. We attend First Assembly of God in Harrisonburg and are involved with children's ministries. I was home-schooled and we named our school "Mountaintop Christian Accadamy." My interests/hobbies are hiking, camping, fishing, photography, horses, skiing, reading, speaking, the arts, praying/interceding for others, missions, and loving Jesus. I have two black pets, a dog named Cinders and a cat named Mulan, each with their own cute personalities. I've been on twenty-one mission trips with my parents, nineteen times to Mexico, once to the Philippines, and once to Turkey, each being quite memorable and enjoyable. It was during this time that God called me to foreign missions, and that's my calling on this Earth—to reach this lost and dying world with the Gospel of Jesus Christ. That's my life story and purpose.

Hidden Talent: Creative arts.

Word or phrase most often overused: You know what I mean?

If you had three wishes, you would want: 1) Wisdom, 2) Favor, and 3) Anointing.

On Friday nights, I usually: Spend time with family and friends.

In ten years, I see myself: Wherever God says.

SARAH, 18
Harrisonburg, Virginia
Hidden Talent: Singing is my passion.
Word or phrase most often overused: Sweet.
If you had three wishes, you would want: More discipline, more patience, and more passion.
On Friday nights, I usually: Watch movies and eat Ben and Jerry's with my two best friends, Kris 'n Kris.
In ten years, I see myself: Hopefully serving the Lord on the stage, but we'll see what He has to say about that.

SEAN C. STEPHENSON, 24
La Grange, Illinois
Sean Clinch Stephenson's appearance, accomplishments, attitude, and physical ability are not typical for a young adult. When he was born, the doctors told his parents that he wouldn't even survive the first night. Now, over two decades later, Sean is traveling across the nation working with leaders ranging from student-government presidents to the president of the United States. While in high school, Sean entertained television audiences by producing, directing, and writing award-winning talk shows, soap operas, dating games, and political interviews. Prior to his current involvement in the field of personal development, Sean's focus was government. Being elected out of a thousand boys to the office of governor (at Illinois Boys State) was an experience that sparked his political curiosity. Following his election to governor, Sean was appointed by the American Legion to represent Illinois in the elite youth organization Boys Nation, an honor reserved for only ninety-six individuals out of 38,000. During his education in political science at DePaul University, Sean spent his summers working with the highest officials in the nation's capital. While working for his mentor, Congressman

William O. Lipinski, on Capitol Hill, Sean learned about democracy up close and personal. After his experience with Congress, Sean moved on to the executive branch. During his stay at the White House, Sean assisted the president, vice president, and cabinet secretaries as an intern for the Office of Cabinet Affairs. Although politics remain in his heart, Sean's true allegiance is to inspirational speaking and writing. At an early age, Sean realized his calling was to help people overcome their obstacles and maximize their lives. By the time he was twenty, he had addressed numerous schools, business, hospitals, foundations, and government agencies. As the CEO of his own company, Sean is touching the lives of thousands ranging in age from kindergartners to corporate executives. Sean attributes his own success to both emotional and physical mastery. Sean most definitely has far surpassed society's expectations of a physically-challenged youth. This is because everyday he defies the odds of his rare bone disorder, osteogenesis imperfecta, which has stunted his growth, caused his bones to be brittle (fracturing over 200 times), and limited his mobility to a wheelchair. Visit Sean online at: www.seanstephenson.com.

Hidden Talent: I can hip-hop dance better than any guy in a popular boy band!

Word or phrase most often overused: I NEVER NEVER NEVER NEVER overuse words.

If you had three wishes, you would: 1) Clean up the world's pollution. 2) Send me an unlimited amount of money. 3) End all human illness and disease.

On Friday nights, I usually: Speak to kids on the importance of loving life and inspiring them to live their dreams.

In ten years, I see myself: A national celebrity that is all over the media, with more money than I could ever spend. This way I could just teach and inspire millions of people and I would never have to think about money again.

THOMAS, 19

Kennett Square, Pennsylvania

God is great. I grew up in the Delaware Valley. I come from a very supportive family. Had great friends and great experiences. Went to college at William and Mary and had more of the same. Just living it up for Jesus each and every day.

Hidden Talent: Knot tying.

Word or phrase most often overused: "Freaking A," and "that's awesome."

If you had three wishes, you would want: Chance to see Jesus in action, the ability to fix the world's problems, a spaceship.

On Friday nights, I usually: Chill with friends.

In ten years, I see myself: Working in the government somewhere.

Printed in the United States
1427000003B/59